# LIFE AT BURGHLEY

*The South View of Burghley House belonging to the Right Honourable Brownlow Cecil Earl of Exeter. Drawn By John Haynes A.D. 1755.*

In 1755 the 9th Earl commissioned John Haynes, a York surveyor, to make plans and drawings of the house and park. This is Haynes's view from the south.

# LIFE AT BURGHLEY
## *Restoring One of England's Great Houses*

by

Lady Victoria Leatham

Little, Brown and Company
Boston · Toronto · London

First American Edition

First published in Great Britain 1992 by The Herbert Press Ltd

Library of Congress Cataloging-in-Publication Data

Leatham. Victoria, Lady.
    Life at Burghley: Restoring One of England's Great
    Houses/ Lady Victoria Leatham.—
    1st ed.
      p.    cm.
    ISBN 0–316–51846–8
      1. Stamford (England)—Social life and customs. 2. Leatham,
Victoria. Lady—Homes and haunts—England—Stamford. 3. Burghley
House (Stamford. Lincolnshire)—History. 4. Country homes—England—
Stamford—History. 5. Manors—England—Stamford—History.
6. Stamford (England)—Biography. 7. Cecil family. I. Title.
DA690, S8L43   1992
942.5'35—dc20                                        92—10739

10 9 8 7 6 5 4 3 2 1

Published simultaneously in Canada by Little, Brown
& Company (Canada) Limited

Printed in Hong Kong

# CONTENTS

# ACKNOWLEDGEMENTS

I owe thanks to a great many people who, in one way or another, have helped me with the writing of this book. In particular, I am grateful to the following: Jon Culverhouse, Sarah Culverhouse, Dr Eric Till, Dr Oliver Impey, Lady Romayne Brassey, Mrs Robin Leigh-Pemberton, Anthony Forbes, the BHPT trustees, Lady Angela Oswald and Sir Giles Floyd Bt.

## PHOTOGRAPHIC ACKNOWLEDGEMENTS

The publishers and author would like to thank English Life Publications Ltd, Derby for permission to use the photographs reproduced on the following pages:
61, 81, 82, 84, 85, 91, 92, 93, 96, 101 (right), 129, 132, 133, 136–7, 140, 141, 144, 146, 147, 151, 154, 155, 158, 159, 162, 163, 164, 165, 166–7, 168, 169, 172–3, 174, 175, 178–9, 183, 186, 187, 218, 222. They are also grateful to the Trustees of the Sir John Soane's Museum for permission to reproduce the two plans on page 74.

Mary Cheke (1) = William Cecil, Lord Burghley, KG (1520–1598) = (2) Mildred Cooke

Dorothy Nevill = Thomas, 1st Earl of Exeter, KG (1542–1622)    Robert Cecil, 1st Earl of Salisbu

William, 2nd Earl of Exeter (1566–1640)    Sir Richard Cecil (1570–1633) = Elizabeth Cope    The Marquesses of Salisbury,
(d.s.p.)                                                                                       of Hatfield House

David, 3rd Earl of Exeter (d. 1643) = Lady Elizabeth Egerton

John, 4th Earl of Exeter (1628–1678) = Lady Frances Manners

John, 5th Earl of Exeter (1648–1700) = Lady Anne Cavendish

John, 6th Earl of Exeter (1674–1721) = Elizabeth Brownlow

John, 7th Earl of Exeter (1700–1722)    Brownlow, 8th Earl of Exeter (1701–1754) = Har

Laetitia Townshend (1) = Brownlow, 9th Earl of Exeter (1725–1793) = (2) Anne Cheatham    Tho

Emma Vernon (1) = Henry, 10th Earl a

Lady Mary Montagu Douglas Scott (1) = David, 6th Marquess of Exeter, KCMG (19

John (d. an infant)    Lady Davina = 11th Lord Barnard    Sir Giles Floyd Bt. (1) = Lady Gillian = (2) George Kertesz    Lad

Hon. Harry Vane    Hon. Carolyn Vane    Hon. Elizabeth Vane    Hon. Sophia Vane    Hon. Louise Vane    David Floyd

# THE CECILS OF BURGHLEY

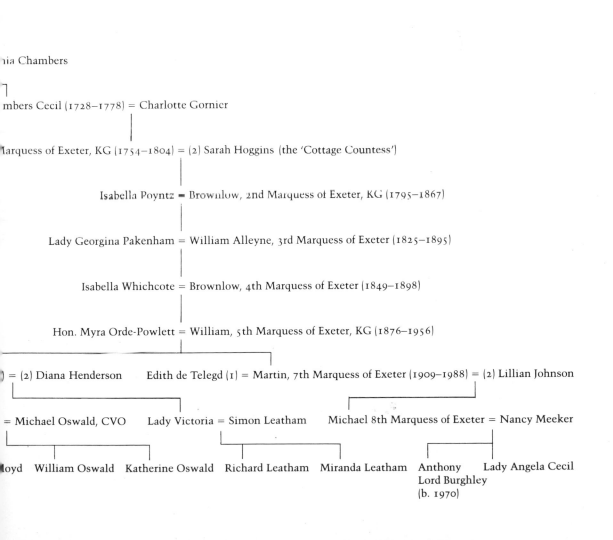

...iia Chambers

...mbers Cecil (1728–1778) = Charlotte Gornier

...larquess of Exeter, KG (1754–1804) = (2) Sarah Hoggins (the 'Cottage Countess')

Isabella Poyntz = Brownlow, 2nd Marquess of Exeter, KG (1795–1867)

Lady Georgina Pakenham = William Alleyne, 3rd Marquess of Exeter (1825–1895)

Isabella Whichcote = Brownlow, 4th Marquess of Exeter (1849–1898)

Hon. Myra Orde-Powlett = William, 5th Marquess of Exeter, KG (1876–1956)

...) = (2) Diana Henderson     Edith de Telegd (1) = Martin, 7th Marquess of Exeter (1909–1988) = (2) Lillian Johnson

... = Michael Oswald, CVO     Lady Victoria = Simon Leatham     Michael 8th Marquess of Exeter = Nancy Meeker

...loyd   William Oswald   Katherine Oswald   Richard Leatham   Miranda Leatham   Anthony   Lady Angela Cecil
Lord Burghley
(b. 1970)

For Simon, Miranda, Richard,
and the Ancestors

*View of the house from the southwest*

CHAPTER ONE

# HOUSE AND HOME

## THE BEGINNING

I WAS NINE YEARS OLD when I first saw Burghley. We arrived in the dark of an October evening and all that I could see of the house was the silhouette of the chimneys and turrets against the sky. But the flaring gas lights at the drive entrance brought home an important fact; in 1956 Burghley still had no electricity.

My parents, my half-brother Anthony Forbes and I were moving into the family home following the death of my grandfather. Until this moment I had not realized that we were moving house for ever; no one had thought to tell me. Nonetheless, it all seemed to be important and exciting. Because of my father's job as Master of Foxhounds with the East Sussex and subsequently the Old Berks, we were fairly used to moving into different homes, but at first glance this imposing castellated family seat was rather surprising and certainly a radical change from the red-brick comfortable modern house we had lived in near Wantage.

Standing on the doorstep to meet us was a grand and upright individual, Mr Groves the butler, the first of the species I had ever encountered. He regarded me with disdain. Children, in his view, were a pesky nuisance. 'Welcome to Burghley M'Lord, M'Lady, Lady Victoria ...' It was the first time anyone other than my parents, teasing, had used the title 'Lady'; it sounded very odd.

The hall was hung with dark crimson damask, and white pilasters reached from the marbled floor to the ceiling. The heavy curtains, used as much to banish draughts as enhance the decor, were of wonderful faded thick chenille and smelt splendidly of dust. Sadly, when with my husband and children I moved back to Burghley in 1982 following my father's death, our labrador ate them.

The first meal in the house was a proper tea. Sandwiches, drop scones, two sorts of cake. We ate it in the dining room, which was divided into three by huge lacquer screens – tea and breakfast in one bit, lunch and dinner in the middle section and Mr Groves breathing like a grampus behind the other screen where the food came in and out from the kitchen.

The whole place appeared enormous; the only comparison I had was the Grosvenor House Hotel, where we stayed when we went to London. Burghley was much darker, more mysterious and more fun. There was a constant hissing from the gas lights and a heavy sweetish smell pervaded the building. In suspect spots in the corridors leaking gas would make a lit match flare up, threatening the eyebrows and encouraging pyromania among children. But the smell was not just the gas, it was a combination of leather books, polish, dust, old dogs. The house exuded age and, unlike Mr Groves, was, I think, rather pleased to see us.

The house and estate were then in need of considerable attention. It was my mother in particular who tackled the vast problems within the house. Nobody had decorated much since World War I. I remember seeing what is now our drinks cupboard, between the sitting room and the drawing room, jammed full of green and foul-smelling medicine bottles. Rooms were furnished in 1930s style. Furniture was displayed in the most extraordinary way and everything needed repair. The hundreds of pictures that my grandfather had enthusiastically coated with poppyseed varnish were now black and shiny. There were tattered textiles and broken porcelain as far as the eye could see. My grandmother had the habit of retrieving any broken piece of porcelain, parcelling it up, and writing on the label 'Broken by Lady X, on 4 August 1939' ... 'Dropped carelessly by Susan in the passage, 12 July' etc.

I have almost forgotten the energy that went into the metamorphosis of such a muddle into a welcoming family home. It is so easy to believe that the repairs you are yourself doing are the first. My mother was a very talented person and the influence of her style of interior decoration is still in the house today.

In addition to doing up the house, my mother had to tackle the staff. Mr Groves had for years reigned crustily supreme in the butler's pantry. In what is now our kitchen, he sat in what was then called 'The Waiting Room', passing idle afternoons ensconced in a sheltering porter's chair, smoking black shag tobacco in a vile pipe and reading penny-dreadfuls. Woe betide anyone who disturbed his relaxation. My grandfather, taking a short cut through with a distinguished guest, was rounded on with 'What do *you* want?' and retreated apologetically through the malodorous

*The Second George Room showing Queen Victoria's bed in 1953 (Country Life)*

cloud to fresher climes. The mutual bad relations between Groves and me were forever sealed by the first grand dinner I attended at Burghley. Faced for the first time in my life with a solid silver soup plate, I leant across to my father (shades of *The Little Princess*) and enquired gloomily 'Are we so poor now that we have to eat off tin?' I heard the grampus mutter behind my chair, 'Stupid child', as he handed round the mulliga-tawny.

When Mr Groves retired we had a few butlers who came and went. There was Mr Glitheroe, ex-RAF and very dashing with white gloves. There was James, who put on his application form, 'Of 5ft 2ins and good appearance' – and so he was. His amiable nephew Raymond came to help; he grinned a lot, especially when, like a bombshell, Heather and Ivy joined the staff as maids. They were extremely nice and beautiful girls from St Helena and with her usual eye for clothes, my mother dressed them in dark red dresses with crisp white aprons. They stood demurely, in shortish skirts, behind my mother's chair in the dining room, just where my father could see them. He beamed contentedly at their glamorous addition to the eighteenth-century room, and the house was enormously cheered by their giggles and charm.

Sometime after Mr Glitheroe, about 1960, Jim Curtis became butler. He had begun life at Burghley as a footman working for my grandparents and was much in demand on the rare occasions that the state coach was used because of his beautiful legs. He looked splendid on the running board. He married one of the housemaids, Edna, who had worked for my grandmother and remembers the State Rooms being used during shooting parties. Edna later became my mother's lady's maid. She and Jim amassed between them thirty-five years in service at Burghley and continued to help with the shooting parties held in the 1980s, and, until Jim's un-timely death in 1990, they both used to steward in the State Rooms on a Sunday. When we moved into Burghley in 1982 Jim was a great influence and help to us all. We miss him more than ever as time goes by; he was part of Burghley.

It was during Jim Curtis's time in charge that the incident with Paddy occurred. Paddy was an ageing and engaging Irishman who came as number two in the pantry. He was rather fond of drink and, in order to counteract its obvious effects, took pills of some description. One day he was deputed to bring in the main course at lunch, and while Jim was pouring wine there was an enormous crash from beyond the door. We all froze and Jim went to inspect the damage. Coming back to my mother, he hissed in a penetrating whisper 'M'Lady, M'Lady, Paddy's gone again'. Faced with the sort of crisis she excelled at, my mother went to investigate, followed by the assembled company. Lying senseless on the stone floor was Paddy in a welter of chicken suprême. With presence of mind Mama removed his teeth and undid his trouser buttons, which was fine until he regained consciousness and stood up, whereupon his trousers fell down, and he could not speak.

Before Edna, my mother's lady's maid was Miss Scriven. She was rather grand – people said she was quality that fate had cast down. She was very kind to me, and fascinated me with her broad Birmingham accent. She was fond of gin and paid the 'roof man' two pounds a week to

*The Burghley state coach in London for the coronation of King George VI in 1937, with C. Peckitt and J. Curtis as footmen, and Captain Townsend as driver*

*Jim and Edna Curtis*

clear away the empties from her room (via the window that gave onto the leads) so as to avoid gossip. When we moved here in 1982 we opened a door of one of the turrets on the roof and were nearly bowled over by an avalanche of Gordon's Gin bottles. The roof man was in charge of gutters, clearing them of leaves and moss, watching for fire, and in the depths of winter was responsible for preventing the downspouts from freezing up. In retrospect he was perhaps something of an anachronism, but frequently since his retirement we have mourned his absence when water cascades through ceilings due to a blocked drain or snowed-up gutter.

A crucial person in the life of the household was Walter Barnes the chauffeur. He taught first my aunts and then me to drive. This was a scary process in the case of Aunt Winifred Hotham. Her eyesight was never very good, and he confided to me his terror when, peering through the windscreen, she asked, 'Is that car coming towards us or going away from us, Barnes?' On being told it was approaching, she said 'Oh, my God' and shot straight off the road into the hedge.

*Walter Barnes, the chauffeur, driving HM The Queen in 1962*

Many of the staff who were here when I was young were characters. For example, Mr Giddings and his wife, who lived in a metal wartime pre-fab called, appealingly, Belsen. It had no inside bathroom, and my mother, appalled, had one installed immediately she arrived. I was with her when we met Mrs Giddings on the drive: 'How is the bathroom Mrs Giddings?' asked my mother, 'It's a bloody disaster M'Lady', rather unexpectedly came the response. 'Bloody Giddings, in there from morning to night, singin to isself in the bloody bath, e's like a bloody goldfish.' Rather chastened we moved off, and I remember my mother saying under her breath, 'And I bet he wears his cap in the bath.' (Mr Giddings's cap was well known for its vile appearance and was seemingly glued to his head.) In later years Mrs Giddings worked in the cafeteria; her language was always colourful, and her tendency to feed me on freshly baked goodies greatly endeared her to me.

Beset by death duties and horrific maintenance costs on the building itself, my parents took the decision when we moved to Burghley to open the house to the public. We followed a trend set by Longleat and Woburn, to name but two other great houses, but we did not go down the safari park/funfair trail. Papa always said the product was so good it could stand on its own without any frills. However, a rather ghastly kiosk, selling transfer printed ashtrays and crested spoons, sprang up in the yard by the back door. Loos, so overwhelmingly hideous that they would not be tolerated now, were installed, and a cafeteria was fitted out in Capability Brown's eighteenth-century orangery, painted primrose and blue, with all the staff in matching overalls. The Scottish wife of the Hunt Secretary Reg Hobbs gamely ran the 'caff', as it was known, courtesy of Mrs Giddings. Grace Hobbs was one of the best cooks I have ever known, with a flair for pastry and scones wonderful to behold. The 'caff' was heaven for children with its milk shakes and fantastic banana lollies. She was succeeded by Mrs Schofield, whose language was worse than Mrs Giddings's but who also had a soft spot for children and gave us food with as much enthusiasm as her predecessor.

The 'caff' also provided much entertainment and pleasure for my mother whose particular province it was. I think that people were not a little astonished by her taking their orders and carrying trays. She once came back to the house triumphantly bearing two shillings, her tips for waiting on tables during the afternoon.

In fact both my parents enjoyed opening the house to the public; Papa was a very friendly man and loved talking to people on their tour round. When he died I had some wonderful letters from visitors whose day had been cheered up by his sense of humour and his seeming ability to walk through walls; in reality the inner walls of the State Rooms have well-concealed doors, but they do make people jump. Papa also used to sit on a Sunday gazing out of the dining room window with occasional yells of 'A fiver', or more frequently, 'Ten bob', as he watched the tourists watching him.

The first guidebook to the house had been written by a local clergyman in the nineteenth century when visitors, by prior arrangement, could be shown round the house by the housekeeper. They were not charged for the visit but the guide book cost 3/6d and they were encouraged to buy. The next edition was issued, I believe, in my grandparents' time. It still bore the legend 'The park has recently been laid out by the ingenious hand of Mr Brown', without mentioning that it was more than one hundred years since Capability Brown had transformed the park. When the modern opening of the house took place in 1956, it was obvious that a new guidebook was needed. My parents and my brother-in-law, Sir Giles Floyd, set to with no experience whatsoever and in the shortest possible time produced a creditable effort which was still in use in 1981. When I was earning pocket money guiding in the house during the school holidays, I memorized sections of the book, including artists' names. This has had a very disconcerting effect on my ability to remember newly attributed information, as though the little grey cells are saying, 'don't believe her, she's done this to us before'.

Re-attribution of the pictures was part of my father's contribution to the re-organization of the house. Paintings were his passion. He had inherited from his mother a love and fascination for the collection which meant many happy hours corresponding with museum personnel abroad, and often involved them coming to Burghley to re-attribute the pictures, wrongly labelled in the last century. One instance of dotty labelling can cause an entire collection to be regarded with suspicion by the experts. This is what happened at Burghley and my father did his best with current information to put it right. At one point we were festooned with Raphaels and Leonardo da Vincis, whether by mischievous design or mischance I am not sure, but since about 1965 we have been de-Rembranted, de-Titianed and de-Raphaeled, to name but a few, which is painful and rather disconcerting. The only good thing to come out of it all is that we now know that we have the greatest collection of seventeenth-century Italian artists' works known to have been bought for one house and showing the taste of a seventeenth-century nobleman.

My father employed a Dr Happ as picture restorer. He had come to

England as a refugee and had come to us highly recommended. The elegant library on the ground floor was converted into his studio and here he kept his vast containers of spirit, turpentine, methyl alcohol and resins. One by one the paintings went in there for restoration. Dr Happ joined us everyday for lunch. There would be a knock on the door, the heavy breathing of a chain smoker and then he would appear. It used to annoy my mother that he always knocked on the open door before entering, even after he had been working here for about three years. He was going bald and had fallen into the terrible trap of parting his hair just above one ear, winding the resulting strand round his scalp and glueing it down with pomade. His teeth were blackened with nicotine, but his appetite was excellent, and we would finish long before he ingested his last morsel. He spoke poor English, and if you told him a piece of news, he would say 'Aow naow' in a voice of amazement. It became a game to see how many 'Aow naows' we could make him say in one meal. He was in fact a very kind man and took me on as a pupil restorer when I left school, though my drawing was so bad that we parted company.

When we moved to Burghley in 1956 my father's main preoccupations were the problems of a virtually bankrupt estate and getting the hunting sorted out. In the ten or so years before our move, my father had been employed as Master of Hounds, first to the East Sussex and then to the Old Berks. He adored his hunting. A highly competent and enthusiastic sportsman, he hunted hounds for the joy of the 'venery', the business of being involved in nature, watching for changes in the wind, examining the rides and tracks in woods to see if there was evidence of 'Charley' having passed that way. One of my earliest memories is of lying flat above an earth, listening to the battle raging eighteen inches below between an old dog fox and a terrier. My father disliked digging foxes out, but on this occasion he was under a lot of pressure because twenty-two assorted bantams and hens belonging to my mother had been murdered by this old predator, and Papa's life would not have been worth living if the guilty party had not been despatched.

As soon as practicable, my father came to an arrangement to hunt part of the Fitzwilliam and part of the Cottesmore countries. These were generous offers on both sides, and offers that meant he could have his private pack of Burghley foxhounds. A charming man called Reg Hobbs came up from the Old Berks to be Hunt Secretary. With his help, and that of Will Garrett, the kennel huntsman, a pack of hounds, donated by

21

friends, was established in the bottom yard. Along with the hounds came horses, nineteen of them at the peak of operations, all clipped and fit and ready for the family and the hunt servants. The thought of what it must have cost does not bear examination. The stable yard was always full of bustle and activity, with various whippers-in who came and learnt their trade and went on to better things. Stable boys soon mastered the art of climbing back over the wall after the gates were locked at 11 p.m.

All this was something of a change from the stables as they were run when we arrived. They were managed then by a little bow-legged gnome-like man with a damson nose who whistled between his teeth, called Mr Gillies. My grandfather, towards the end of his life, had reduced the number of horses and Mr Gillies spent his time tending the two brood mares in the bottom-yard stables, both of whom were demented as a result of being incarcerated within a high-walled enclosure. Mr Gillies sat in the tack room, full of polished equipment and heated by a cylindrical coal-fired stove which made the all-pervading smell of saddle

*John Hill, groom, with Dizzy, one of the family ponies, at the turn of the century*

*(opposite above) Reg Hobbs (extreme left) standing next to Will Garrett (mounted) at the opening meet in 1966*

*(opposite below) The Stable courtyard, designed by Capability Brown*

soap even more pungent. Included here was all the old harness from the days of the coach and four, silver-mounted, and in keeping with the crested pale blue horse blankets. Most of the tack was subsequently stolen, together with rare bits and bridles dating back to the nineteenth century. One delightful little throwback to a previous era was a basket-work saddle-seat, used when they were young by my father, his brother and sisters on an enormously overweight and hairy Shetland pony. I am grateful that whoever liberated the rest of the tack left this – a real heirloom.

*H. Pepper, Head Keeper and Cecil Pepper's father*

Another figure I remember from these sporting years was Cecil Pepper. Keeper at Burghley all his life, succeeding his father before him, he was tiny and lean, had large blue eyes and a very high pitched voice. He hunted on a most noble beast; about seventeen-hands high, with a wild eye and flaring nostrils. Mr Pepper bounced around on top of this huge animal, brandishing his hunting crop and exhorting the hounds to behave in a rather squeaky voice. He was twice married. The first Mrs Pepper was terribly adenoidal and I recall my mother going to see her and sympathizing with her terrible cold: 'Oh bo, B'Lady,' said Mrs P cheerily, 'It's be adedoids.' In later years, after her death, and before he married again, I heard that Mr Pepper was caught 'in flagrante' in the long grass down by the old stables. I don't know who was the more surprised, the catcher or the caught.

## MY FATHER

IN ADDITION TO INHERITING this wonderful Elizabethan house, my father was also possessor of the titles Marquess of Exeter, Hereditary Grand Almoner and Lord Paramount of the Soke of Peterborough – enough for anyone to be going on with. He was, however, better known as David Cecil, Lord Burghley, one of the golden athletes of his generation. All those who saw the film *Chariots of Fire* will recall the young aristocrat played by Nigel Havers. He was portraying my father. How the eldest son of a Marquess with no genetic reason to take up an athletics career should win a gold medal for Britain at the 1928 Olympics baffled everyone, including himself.

Papa began to win races at Ludgrove, his prep school. In true gentlemanly fashion it was considered thoroughly praiseworthy to excel at sport of any kind, as long as it did not make you bumptious. When he was older Papa did some of his athletic training either at Burghley or on the sports field in the town. I was told a charming story of how, one hot summer's day in 1928, a Green Keeper was mowing the football pitch in Stamford. A young man whom he recognized as Lord Burghley came up and asked for his help in putting up some hurdles. 'Certainly', came the reply. So, together, chatting the while, they arranged the hurdles round the field. My father then did something strange. He placed several empty match boxes on end on top of the hurdles. (By the time *Chariots of Fire*

25

*My father hurdling in the 1920s*

was made these had been transformed into champagne glasses.) He then went to the 'start' and began to practise, trying not to knock the boxes off, as a knocked hurdle costs time. He practised for an hour and then stacked the hurdles away. The Green Keeper remembered asking him where he was running next. 'Oh, I leave for Amsterdam and the Olympics the day after tomorrow' came the reply. He returned with the gold medal for the 400 metres hurdles.

Granny kept every newspaper cutting relating to his athletic career. She must have been fiercely proud of his achievements, although she and my grandfather did not often go to watch him perform. It might have looked rather over keen. However, they did go, with his fiancée Lady Mary Montagu Douglas Scott, as well as his sister Romayne, to watch him compete in Amsterdam. Granny wrote in her diary: 'Today David was carried shoulder high round the stadium in Amsterdam having won the 400 metres hurdles, and gained a gold medal for Britain, truly a moment worth waiting for.'

The public adored him; he epitomized the golden youth of the nation. Fair haired, bright, totally unspoilt, his success was Britain's success. One of his proudest achievements was his victory in 1927 over the clock at Trinity College, Cambridge. Indeed, he was as proud of this as he was of his gold medal. He undertook to race round the paved stone flags of Great Court while the clock was striking twelve. Hundreds of undergraduates and others gathered as the minutes ticked by before the first stroke of noon. Round he went and squeaked home as the last 'dong' rent the air. (Since then Sebastian Coe and Steve Ovett have tried to beat his record and failed.) In the film *Chariots of Fire* Harold Abrahams was depicted as the winner but this was not correct. My father was most upset that history should be misrepresented while there were still people alive who remembered how things had actually been, and fell out badly with David Puttnam, the director of the film, over this. The great authority on the event is Henry Button of Cambridge, a steadfast supporter of my father and a stalwart writer to inaccurate newspaper reporters, setting the record straight.

Papa competed in the 1932 Los Angeles Olympics, ran in the Harvard and Penn University Relays and made many American friends. The lack of any 'side' or pomposity on his part – and, it has to be said, the very fact that the sport had no possibility of financial gain – created a special atmosphere. The parties the athletes had within the discipline of training were prodigious. An American fellow-athlete wrote in his memoirs that some of the best fun he had was when he and my father shared a room on tour. Having overcome the fact that his roommate was a 'real live limey lord' he was astounded by the fact that Papa used 'suspenders' (braces) to hold up his tracksuit bottoms. I remember being told another amusing incident from my father's athletic activities in North America: one of the great sports commentators at Toronto watching the un-fancied Englishman run was so spellbound that he forgot to turn off the microphone switch and a stadium full of people heard him exclaim in wonder, 'Jesus, just watch that bugger Burghley go'!

My father's athletic achievements also included the record for running a quarter mile round the promenade deck of the *Queen Mary*. He did this in 58 seconds, dressed in formal evening wear, in March 1936, on a voyage before the liner went into service. The world record for that distance was then 49.6 seconds, so it was pretty good going; a brass plate was affixed to the deck to commemorate the event.

Once he had retired from active sport my father reckoned it was time to give something back and worked hard for amateur ideals within the Olympic movement for about forty-five years. As President of the International Amateur Athletic Federation, Chairman of the British Olympic Association and a member of the International Olympic Committee he was instrumental in bringing the Olympic Games to England in 1948 and was Chairman of the Organising and Executive Committee for the Games. He persuaded the King to support the event, although there was much difficulty over this because of my father's divorce and re-marriage, which was probably also the reason why he was never decorated for his lifetime's service to sport.

My father's delight in speed was also evident in his driving. He was a frightful driver, far too fast and prone not to use his rear-view mirror. He terrified my mother so much that when we went on holiday to Europe in the car, she would take a pill and lie senseless on the back seat. He perfected the sick-making art of rocking from the brake to the accelerator and to this day I cannot abide the smell of leather upholstery. When he narrowly avoided accidents, he would gaze out of the window and whistle tunelessly between his teeth while my mother yelled imprecations at him from the back seat. I firmly believe that bad driving is inherited ... Papa got it from his mother, who once drove herself and two friends into a ditch in the park. The car was wrecked but the occupants were fine, except for granny whose false teeth flew out and were discovered embedded in the bank.

My father's early driving practice took place long before the days of tests, and involved two vehicles, one called Boneshaker and the other Screaming Jane. He used to make his sister, poor Aunt Winifred, push him up slippery hills. In latter years he had a number of accidents, some on the main road to London, and at least one in Parliament Square. Coming out of the House of Lords, he made contact with a van. Pulling into the side of the road to exchange details with the driver, he explained in self defence, 'My wife was obscuring my view', a gross calumny on my mother who was in her seat doing no harm to anybody. The policeman at the House of Lords became so tired of Papa backing into his motorbike that he tucked his bike in behind a bollard. Papa reversed into the bollard, pushing it back into the bike and breaking the mirror.

At one point a wonderful car appeared in the Burghley garage – an E-type Jaguar, with the numberplate FOX 999. It was very fast and Papa was never really in control. Coming down from London with him one day I enquired how fast it would go. I could see him wrestling with temptation. 'If I show you, you are not to tell your mother!' I promised and he put his foot down. We were doing 125 miles an hour when he lost his nerve and slowed down; it was a delicious secret between us thereafter.

One evening after a particularly wet and muddy day's hunting, we were on our way home when we found two lost hounds … 'Come along Ranger, come along Placid, in you come.' Now the interior of an E-type is not over large and here we were with two unspeakably smelly hounds, all claws and vile breath, jammed into that crazy car. With most of the windscreen obscured by hound and my father unable to change gear without much commotion, it was a nightmare journey. Shortly afterwards he admitted defeat and disposed of the car; the smell lingered still.

## MY MOTHER

My MOTHER WAS STRIKING TO LOOK AT, six feet tall, fair haired and enormous fun. Very popular with many friends, she led a 'gay life' in the old fashioned sense of the word.

In 1929 my father had married the beautiful Lady Mary Montagu Douglas Scott, by whom he had three daughters: Davina who married Lord Barnard, Gillian now married to George Kertesz, having previously been married to Sir Giles Floyd, and Angela married to Michael Oswald. However, the only son, John, so needed to carry on the line, died of meningitis at the age of eighteen months. When Papa married my mother, I am certain that he was hoping for a son. What happens? Another blooming daughter!

I am not sure exactly when the affair between Papa and my mother began. There is no doubt that a strong mutual attraction had existed between them for many years prior to their marriage. I believe they both fought it. They were only too aware of the problems that lay ahead. My mother was widowed in the war. Her husband, Lt-Col David Forbes, was killed commanding a battalion of the Coldstream Guards at Anzio, leaving her with two young children to bring up on her own, Rosemary and Anthony. She also lost two brothers in the war. Her own contribution to the war effort was working in an armaments factory.

29

My father was divorced from his first wife in 1946, in a period when divorce was abhorrent to many people, especially when it affected children and a national idol was involved. The newspapers, instead of containing items about a distinguished athletics career, now related gossip and scurrilous stories. It was unimaginable that my grandparents, within their rigid moral standards, could have coped and they did not. Public and private sympathy were entirely with Mary and the girls. Papa and his new wife were never invited to Burghley. Only when granny was ninety-two did she agree to meet my mother and me. The two of them got on rather well. I never saw my grandfather. Looked at in the light of modern behaviour it all seems incredible.

I cannot imagine how Mama must have felt over her exclusion from Burghley. I am sure that she was well aware that a hostile attitude would be widespread among friends of Papa's family, estate employees and local worthies. Perhaps it was a relief not to have to face them and justify herself to them.

Gradually the relationship between Papa and his parents improved and Mary generously encouraged my half-sisters to visit their father and stepmother. When I was growing up at Tilton in Sussex I remember my half-sister Angela patiently teaching me to tie bows in my shoe laces and Gill reading to me. I once went back with them to stay at Mary's house. She was always terribly kind to me and I was very fond of her. The last time we met was when she attended Papa's memorial service at the Guards' Chapel. I believe she still loved him.

My half-sister Rosemary Leigh-Pemberton was the archetypal elder sister, always adored, who very satisfactorily produced a marvellous nephew for me when I was only seven. Anthony Forbes was always a bit of a star, revered not only by me (once I had got over hating him at age six of course) but by all children including my own. One of the great excitements for Miranda and Richard was going to church to listen to 'Uncle A' singing in his 'growly voice'. In reality a superb bass, he has been known to perform solos at the Christmas carol concert here, but under extreme duress. Both Rosemary and Anthony were fond of my father and he in turn thought a great deal of them, making Anthony one of his executors and a Burghley trustee.

*My father with his first wife*
*and daughters (l to r Gillian,*
*Angela, Davina) in Bermuda*

*My mother*

## GROWING UP AT BURGHLEY

BURGHLEY WAS A MAGICAL PLACE for a child to grow up. I was away a
good deal of the time, of course, at boarding school. But I remember
now the intense delight as we neared the house when I came home for the
long summer holidays. First it would be the smell of the brickworks at
Peterborough, then the glorious drive up to the front door through the
park with the huge and ancient trees, and the dappled deer watching us
pass. Then, once at the house, the joy of joys – the breathless rush down
the familiar passage to the study where Papa would be sitting at his desk,
with Miss Johns his secretary taking dictation. The dogs would be
everywhere at once, there was the familiar sight of my mother lighting
Turkish cigarettes, and I was happy in the knowledge that for two
glorious months I was back in the place I loved best in all the world.

To reach my room and that of my half-brother Anthony on the top
floor you had to climb a winding staircase of sixty-seven stairs. A torch
was provided but it was thrilling to do it in the dark. Gas lamps hissed at
the bottom and top but in between was dim and shadowed uncertainty.
Coming down one evening in bare feet to say the necessary good nights, I
trod on something warm, furry and unexpected halfway down. I cleared
the final flight in one and arrived gibbering in the sitting room. We armed
ourselves with a torch, and there lying smugly on the stairs was my
mother's mink tippet which had slithered off its hanger on the way to the
wardrobe.

It was wonderful waking up in my room on a summer's morning,
hearing the Canada geese on the lake, jumping out of bed and in shorts,
sandals, T-shirt and no socks, whizzing down to breakfast. Then along to
say good morning to my parents and off to the stables or to my favourite
haunt, the blacksmith's shop. Carl Zimmerman was the blacksmith
then, just as he is today. A delightful man, he and I had great fun when I
was young. I learnt how to make a horseshoe, how to hammer red-hot
metal and how to plunge it into the great tank to cool it. Watching him
shoe a horse was a privilege, and on cold days the heat of the forge was
very consoling. I do not recall ever being bored, as there were always
things to do and people to talk to.

On wet days, when confined inside, it was a rare treat to wander
round the house opening drawers. Every table, every chest held secrets:
letters, bills, pen wipers, bits of lacquer, porcelain dishes and, on one

*The north front, dated 1587, the last part built
by the first Lord Burghley*

occasion, jewellery. This habit of snooping drove my parents crazy, they couldn't bear it when I burst into the room saying excitedly, 'Look what I've found'. It seemed incredible to me that they weren't gripped with fascination. In retrospect I am so glad that they did not succumb to my entreaties, considering the fun we have had since then.

The house became rather good at hosting groups of children playing 'home' in the passages. This game involved much running and hiding between items of furniture while 'it' prowled about looking for victims to kidnap. There was also a challenging activity called 'Round the World' which took place in the inner courtyard where you had to circumnavigate the four sides without touching the ground. As I regard the crumbling stone sills today, I have terrible pangs of conscience that we brought forward the decay by a good few years.

*Winner of the 400 metres hurdles, 30 July 1928, Olympic Games, Amsterdam*

*(opposite) My father, when Lord Burghley, painted in his*
*Cambridge blue dressing gown by Oswald Birley*

*The author as a child*

On several occasions rooms would be given over to serious gambling. Taught *vingt-et-un* by my much loved governess, local friends and cousins took to it like ducks to water. We made very satisfactory coinage with Coca-Cola bottle tops, squashed flat by freight trains which rumbled past on the Peterborough to Leicester line half a mile from the house. My parents too could be persuaded to play on occasion, although my mother was prone to panic, never quite sorting out when to 'buy' and when to 'twist'.

Despite my difficulties with Mr Groves the butler, I became friends with David, his grandson. We made camps in unlikely places and caught inedible perch in the lake. These were unwillingly processed by the cook and appeared in the dining room, very small and tasting of cotton wool, bones and mud.

Reg Hobbs, the Hunt Secretary, tried without success to teach me to ride well. A succession of beastly ponies made certain that I detested riding until I got my first horse, who taught me confidence. Poor Reg, he could not understand fear himself, and underrated its effect on a skinny ten year old.

School holidays came and went. In the winter there were shooting parties which included lovely dinners where all the men wore dinner jackets and velvet smoking jackets and the ladies, relishing the chance to take the family jewels out of the bank, wore diamond brooches which were rather large. However, the jewels were often very black because they had been in the vaults. The women seldom shot, but one, Lady Gault, regularly came to stay and was an excellent markswoman.

Papa drove his Landrover at speed over ploughed fields, quite often getting bogged down and having to be dug out. We used to shoot duck on a local lake called Whitewater, a misnomer if ever there was one. It had smellier mud and water than can be imagined, and sitting in the back of the Landrover on the way home was a real penance. We had a charming but wayward yellow labrador given to us by Dick Poole, a friend of Papa's in Berkshire. In his honour the dog was called Poole. He was totally disobedient and extremely strong, and I can remember watching him tow the Landrover across a field of stubble in pursuit of a fallen bird. He had been lashed to the bumper to stop him running in and the accompanying language was biblical in its intensity as my father, on two sticks, attempted to arrest the vehicle's progress. We were struck motionless and speechless with laughter and unable to help at all.

My father had two hip replacements and then, as a result of continuing hunting against advice, had to have the first one done again. This effectively prevented him riding, so it was a very sad time for the hounds. In 1967, Will Garrett, the kennel huntsman who had been with the Burghley hounds since the beginning, left his wife and the hounds one morning without a word to anyone. We heard the commotion of hungry voices down at the kennels later that morning, and discovered the situation. Naturally, his wife was desolate, but so was my father – to leave

*Carl Zimmerman in the forge*
*(opposite) The west front, dated 1577*

a wife and a job was one thing, but to leave a pack of hounds was quite something else. An excellent replacement was found in Jim Carpenter from the woodyard, to tide things over, but the days of the Burghley Hunt were numbered. The hounds were dispersed to other packs and the horses were sold where possible, although a few brood mares remained to keep alive the passion my father had for the sport. Thankfully the Burghley Three Day Event Horse Trials, held here since 1961, took much of his time and enthusiasm; it flourishes still, a tribute to him.

The house at this time had more or less settled into a routine. The picture restoration was done and we were under the impression that the roof had been repaired. There were the usual excitements in the family:

*My wedding, 1967*

*Miranda's christening, 1970*

weddings, christenings and so on. My parents adopted the granny and grandpa role with gusto, although Burghley was known to one frustrated grandson as 'the don't touch house'. It was certainly a most inconvenient house for tiny babies and those who look after them. The front hall bristled with prams and the day and night nurseries were resurrected on the top floor. It was backbreaking work lugging an enormous carrycot up all those stairs, and highly inconvenient for the nanny to take masses of soggy nappies down to the washroom in buckets, way out of earshot of her bawling charge. I once asked my mother to babysit while we went out to dinner locally. By the time we got home at a very modest 10.30 p.m., she was in a state of total collapse having galloped up and down the stairs at least four times in the evening.

*(overleaf) Burghley from the south lawn. All the second-storey windows in the section between the angle turrets are blanks, disguising the height of the State Rooms*

# CHAPTER TWO

# BURGHLEY TODAY

## TAKING ON THE JOB

WITH MY PARENTS' ADVANCING AGE and the lameness suffered by both of them, management of the house and estate gradually began to decline. The only things that proliferated were wheelchairs. There were two, one a rather racy model with a battery, which whirred along the passages at a decent speed, the other more laid back, propelled by hand. Needless to say, when my mother became just as lame as Papa, if not more so, having fallen down the stairs at Fortnum and Mason, the speedy version was in great demand. They took it in turns. Going along to meals was a military exercise, with the two of them manoeuvring in and out of the furniture, passing much free advice to each other. Corners in the corridors were a hazard and I fear that the boulle took a bit of a hammering. The worst problems occurred when, like Boadicea leading the Iceni into the fray in her chariot with knife blades protruding, a carelessly balanced walking stick across the knees wrought havoc on chair and table legs along the corridor walls.

Not quite so much effort as before was put into the maintenance of the house and collections; an insidious contraction took place. My parents asked less and less of the workforce and an easing of supervision occurred. Repairs were not done with the same sense of urgency as in the past. My father spent most of his time doing fiendishly difficult jigsaw puzzles hired from the jigsaw loan club. When he was not thus engaged, he weeded the lawns of plantains, and tried to decide what should happen to Burghley when he died.

For that, he needed to devise a scheme whereby the Treasury would not force his successor to sell the collections in order to pay 'death duty'. Part of the problem was that he had no son. His younger brother Martin would inherit the title, but he had left England for Canada in 1930 when he was 21, to run a ranch purchased by his father before World War I. Now the spiritual leader of a religious group in British Columbia, it was uncertain that he would want to take on the house and the care of the multitude of works of art within it. My father was adamant on one thing: that nothing should be sold. He had been forced by the death duty payable on his father's estate to sell many items from the house, and he did not want it to happen again. The only solution seemed to be a gift to the National Trust.

For many months the negotiations dragged on, with learned men coming down to look at the contents of the house. There were, however, large areas of disagreement, such as one that emerged when an expert suggested to my mother that all items of furniture in a room should be of the same period. As she had spent most of the previous fifteen years mixing the room contents so that they appeared to be as unlike a museum as possible, this did not go down well. In the end we could not endow the gift with the amount of cash required by the National Trust to prevent it being a drain on their resources, so the idea was dropped.

The scheme finally arrived at by my father is the one in place now. He created a charitable trust to which he gave the parts of the house which were open to the public, together with the contents and an endowment, and he arranged that, on his death, the rest of the house and contents should pass to the Trust. He made it very clear to the trustees that he wanted the house to be lived in, preferably by a member of the family, to avoid it becoming a museum. Apart from the rather sad fact that Burghley would never again belong to a Marquess of Exeter, it was a splendid solution and very innovative at the time.

It was not finally decided who would live in the house. Believing himself to be in pretty good shape physically, apart from his replaced hips, my father saw no reason to suppose that he would not copy his mother, who, sustained on hunting port, lived in Yorkshire until she was ninety-four. However, it was not to be. In October 1981 he was suddenly taken ill in London, and admitted to the King Edward VII hospital at five in the afternoon with a chest pain and breathlessness. I rang the hospital and amazingly was put through to his room. 'Hello darling, your mother has just gone to the flat to get my pyjamas and a bottle of port. Did you see that *Ironside* is on the television?' Somewhat reassured by the cheerfulness of his voice, I nonetheless rang my half-

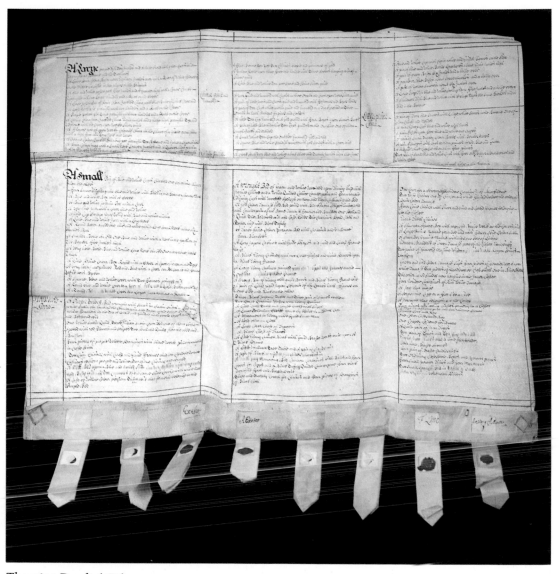

*The 1690 Deed of Gift*

*(opposite) With Simon at Burghley, c.1983, shortly after moving in*

sisters to pass on the news. At about midnight, he died from a massive heart attack. He was seventy-six.

Everyone was expecting my mother to carry on at Burghley on her own, but a month or so after Papa died she rang us up and asked if we could bear the thought of her coming to live at the end of our drive in a 'granny cottage'. She found life at the big house unbearably lonely, and, try as we all did, there was no easy way to remove all the day-to-day management worries from her.

As the days went by it became obvious that she was not at all well. We sent her to her London doctor who diagnosed a 'nervous stomach'. Unconvinced she returned to Burghley, driven as always by Walter Barnes's successor, Colin Shiner, who had become a loyal friend to both my parents. When she arrived back I was at Burghley and was appalled to see that she was terribly jaundiced. The splendid Doctors Hibble and Barker from Stamford took over. She was in Peterborough Hospital by the next day and was diagnosed as having a tumour on her pancreas. In spite of a major operation at the Middlesex Hospital she steadily went

*My parents' mausoleum; 'the trout hatchery'*

downhill, unable to imagine life without her beloved 'Second David' as she called him, and five months later died at Burghley.

The family vault in the church in Stamford was full so both my parents were interred in what became known as 'His Lordship's Trout Hatchery', a mausoleum on the other side of the lake from the house. Designed by my father, it bears a close resemblance to a bus shelter. When it was under construction, a lady house guest went out for a brisk walk. Seeing the excavations in progress, she enquired breezily if this was a new trout hatchery, and was much embarrassed by the reply that it was to be his Lordship's final resting place.

The suddenness of events meant that the trustees found themselves in a tight situation. Faced with an empty house where morale among the staff was at an all-time low, and where works of art were deteriorating, they had to act. My husband Simon and I, and our two children, Miranda and Richard, were living at Alconbury, twenty-five miles from Burghley. I had worked at Sotheby's for a few years and also knew the house at first hand, having grown up there. The request came that we should move in and run the house for the Trust and try to pull it round a bit. We had the very strong impression that events were overtaking us and that life was about to become more complicated and less private. And there was an enormous job to be done which would require every ounce of energy that we possessed.

In retrospect, moving back to Burghley in October 1982 was a nightmare: for Simon, working incredibly hard at his job of chief executive of a shipping finance company in London; for Miranda and Richard, both at Wellesley House school in Kent, who had both adored their grandparents and for whom the idea of living in granny's house, where we could still smell her scent and Turkish cigarettes, was very upsetting; and for me knowing that a great deal of responsibility lay ahead with many people believing we would make a real mess of things.

At the time we were all so busy and strung up by the previous horrendous months, and with the loss of both my parents, that the physical struggle of fitting the contents of our previous home into this one became just one more problem.

Our local removal firm, Steeles of Stamford, had three vans unloading at three different entrances, and coped admirably with my indecisions as well as a force-nine gale, which slammed doors shut just as the men were about to totter through them laden with china lamps. Matters were not helped by the three dogs rushing about, copiously watering internal stone walls. It was going to be hard for them to learn to do otherwise and I wished we had had shares in squeegee mops.

The removers put up with my dotty, but for the most part effective, colour-coded labelling system, which was fine when you knew where the rooms were, but a bit tricky given the size of the building. The men even remained stoically cheerful when I delivered the *coup de grace* – the piano, inevitably, had to go to the top floor. Up the sixty-seven winding stairs they laboured. I felt like a murderer as they wheezed and panted. Muttered curses hung heavy on the air and the situation was not helped by the budding musician, our daughter Miranda, saying with some perplexity, 'Why on earth are you putting it upstairs? I'll never play it up there'. She was quite right; no one has laid a finger on the keys ever since.

Everything which had somehow escaped the fail-safe colour coding system ended up in the South Dining Room; a grandiose and pillared room, already piled high with flower vases, a ping-pong table, two pedal cars and assorted broken furniture. We had no choice but to go right on in and add to the mountain of confusion. It took six years to get it sorted out, and in the interim two nests of rodents established a breeding station down the back of the sofa. Swines! It serves me right for not getting on with the clearing up before.

It was very apparent to Simon and me when we arrived that we were fighting a sort of war. Put another way, the house was like a huge liner which was sailing along without anyone at the helm. It was a matter not just of taking decisions, although that was an important element, but of establishing ourselves as a viable family unit within the household, to whom people could relate for the right reasons. We had to fight against certain old-established practices among the staff. For example, if a light bulb needed changing the custom was for the butler to telephone the house electrician to come and do the job. Or if a heavy table had to be moved, another call would be made, this time to the house carpenter, to ask him to come to the house. Above all, the battle to earn acceptance among everyone in the house had to be fought and won quickly if we were going to get the show on the road. Inevitably there were a few defections from the staff. After all, it was quite a shock to have a youngish couple with two teenage children, three dogs, and outside jobs after the quiet years of my parents. We were prepared to give more, but we also demanded more flexibility and harder work.

It had been my great good fortune, in the years before I took over Burghley, to work for Sotheby's where I had been trained as a 'generalist valuer' in London and then gone on to run the Cambridge office. When the move to Burghley was mooted, I was sure I would lose my job. It is forty-four minutes drive from Burghley to Magdalene Bridge at a cracking pace, and to have to go out on visits from there made it a hopeless proposition. I did it for a while but gave up out of exhaustion. Running the house was, and is, very tiring.

Sotheby's came up with a solution. On a shoestring we opened an office in Stamford, very much for a trial run. We set up shop in the conference centre at the George Hotel where we had a tiny room, with just enough space for my desk and for wonderful, beautiful Polly Newbury, my secretary. Opening the Stamford office was a helpful development as far as the house was concerned. We were in the throes of the usual ghastly business of probate appraisals. Here I was with an army of friends who advised us from the word go on values, insurance, conservation and display, and without whose help I would have been completely sunk. I have had to abandon full-time work, but these friends are still my first line of defence against total immersion in the house, and provide patches of sanity and refuge in the enlarged office in Stamford now run efficiently by George Archdale.

Slowly things began to settle down, but I still felt like an interloper in someone else's house, and I know Simon did too. It would have been an impossible task to sort the house out without his help; it was in no way a one person job. In the kitchen Mrs Collinson, who had been cooking for my parents, saw us into the house and then took her greatly overdue retirement. She was a lovely lady with a glorious sense of humour and unbelievable skills with cottage pie and lemon meringue. We all loved her and missed her terribly.

The kitchen was the dreariest one I have ever cooked in; my only lifeline was the internal telephone on which I could sometimes persuade the children to bring me a strengthening glass of this or that. The kitchen was then about thirty yards from the dining room. A huge cavernous room, freezing in the winter and boiling in the summer, it was fitted with the essential Aga, a terrifying gas range, a commercial potato peeler and two crackled white earthenware sinks. To transport the food from the kitchen to the dining room was an adventure. First you had to prop open the door (circa 1688), then advance into the draughty stone back hall, carefully climb a flight of worn stone stairs, negotiate a locked security door, bypass the rope and stanchion used to restrain the public from joining in the meal, and arrive at the dining room door with the food stone cold and the cook in a foul humour. The butler, Harold Geary, was somewhat disconcerted by my doing the cooking, but he developed a fine technique for when I had galloped up to the dining room. He would sweep grandly through the door bearing the serving dish with a huge silver cover, and, with an air of a *maître d'* in a smart restaurant, would whisk off the cover and announce, 'Roast chicken tonight, M'Lady'. We never quite knew how to react to this startling performance. I hope we looked impressed.

Harold was a star in more ways than one. He was as new at the job of butler as I was at trying to run the house, but he taught me a great deal about how things had been done in the past. Employed originally as a footman, his real name was Leslie not Harold, but when Jim Curtis interviewed him for the job he was told, 'Good Heavens, we can't have a footman called Leslie; we'll call you Harold.'

Because of the inaccessibility of the kitchen, the first radical change we made in our living accommodation was to install the 'Little Chef'. Leading off Simon's dressing room, it had in times past been my father's bathroom. I was not going to waltz down the passage for about a hundred yards, let alone negotiate the stone stairs and the locked door, in order to get to the kitchen to brew up before Simon left for the office at 7.40 a.m. So the 'Little Chef' was born. Tiny, with a fridge, a cooker and a sink, it is ideal and made us feel at home for the first time. It did, however, suffer a setback once when I burnt the toast; a flaming brand shot out of the toaster and set fire to the varnished cork tiles on the wall. When I arrived to pour out the coffee for breakfast I found a scene from *The Towering Inferno*, the room filled with noxious fumes, the whole wall alight and the wretched toaster, the villain of the piece, sitting innocently on the shelf. But a quick squirt with the soda siphon worked wonders and normal play was resumed, if a trifle smokily.

Once the Open Season started we had to get used to the locked doors and occasional break-ins by the public. The children became quite good at herding lost visitors back whence they had come, often apparently unaware that No Entry was an instruction and not a question. People used phenomenal initiative, often vaulting the rose-clad fence designed to confine them to the public part of the garden and, not content with that, even managing to scale the ha-ha. One man arrived one Sunday morning when I was on the terrace quietly writing to my son Richard. He demanded that I should go and pose for a photograph among the rose beds. I enquired of the tattooed and perspiring photographer, clad sportingly in a red vest, how he had reached me? 'Well,' he said chummily, sitting down for a good chat, 'you wouldn't believe the trouble I had getting across that b***** ditch.' I remarked that I was extremely glad to hear it. Looking pained at my lack of enthusiasm for his daring feat, he went on to explain that it had taken the combined efforts of himself, his wife and his mother-in-law to heave him onto the lawn. Now he had arrived he was not going to leave without a photograph. We settled for one with the fountains and he returned to his admiring relations, via the barbed wire of the ha-ha, which he had swathed in a black and fluorescent green jersey to cushion the spikes.

One of our most important tasks was to battle against the decay we saw all around us in the fabric of the building. When we arrived at Burghley, the trustees had already begun the horrendous task of restoring the roof. A huge job. All the careful work done in my father's time had to be undone. Under the outside skin, moisture had become trapped by the chipboard supporting the alloy and terrible rot had attacked the timbers holding up the precious ceilings of the State Rooms. The condensation caused by the breath and bodies of thousands of visitors had risen to the ceilings and caused enormous damage. We realized that we would be entering a period of almost total renovation of the roof structure.

Scaffolding is still up ten years later, and the dramas are played out daily as, with the devoted care of our builders, Bowmans of Stamford, run by Peter Loft, and the house architect, Alan Wilson, we endeavour to give this great edifice another few hundred years.

The grant system for Grade One listed buildings (those of exceptional interest) is fraught with delay and paperwork. The architect employed by English Heritage (the government-funded conservation body with responsibility for the built heritage) to inspect the building changes frequently. Quite often he or she will not have seen a house of this age and size before, will not have been apprized of the activities of the last inspector, and will either have to approve an immensely complicated and costly engineering project, or give the plan the thumbs down, which may mean the building suffering irrevocable damage.

The system of grant aid is a much appreciated and necessary source

*Workmen cutting stone to restore a chimney*

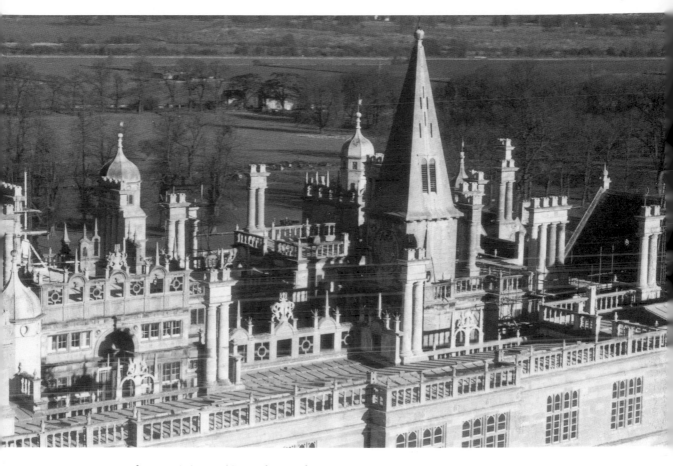

*An aerial view of the roof from the south*

of obtaining funds, but I believe it has to be sharpened up if those houses most in need are to be saved. The financial truths are horrifying. The Burghley House Preservation Trust will have spent well over £100,000 every year for fifteen years by the time the roof is finished. In the past about sixty per cent of the roof-repair costs were met by the Trust and forty per cent by English Heritage. With the smaller allowance now given to English Heritage by the government the percentage has changed, but continued assistance in funding repairs of this nature is vital. With the current economic climate in farming, from which houses like Burghley traditionally receive their revenue, the gap between income and expenditure is widening all the time.

55

Burghley is built on rock. This is fine according to biblical instructions but lightning conductors were obviously not much of a problem in the Holy Land. When we came to check this vital piece of equipment, we found that my ancestors had indeed put in a system. They had attached copper straps to the turrets and weather vanes of the house, then run them to ground on the lead down-spouts. When the lead was replaced with plastic, however, the copper was tied to that instead and there is not much earthing capacity in a plastic pipe.

The real fun and games began when we tried to find soil to a depth of twelve feet next to the house. Not even three feet were there. There was nowhere to bury the ends of the cables where they could discharge a lightning strike safely and we ended up with six copper mats disbursed under the topsoil to discharge sideways.

Internally we embarked on a programme of decoration and restoration. We employed 'Whistling Pete' for a bit. He was a painter and decorator of prodigious speed – he could start and finish a bathroom in a day. Somehow it seemed vital to 'get a crack on' as he called it. The trouble was firstly that his wallpaper tended to peel off within six months, and secondly that he managed, with supreme skill, to paper over the pipes so that strange bulges appeared with air pockets underneath – providing a frightful temptation to put a finger through.

The decoration was vital from a personal point of view, as well as to embellish the house. Our children, Richard and Miranda, had adored their grandparents. It still felt very much granny's house, and as long as the rooms looked as they always had, there was little chance that the family would feel at home. The top floor where I had lived as a child was deputed once again to be the place for the younger generation. It has its advantages; we cannot hear the reverberations of their music. However, because the state rooms are directly underneath, the odd visitor trying to soak up the original Elizabethan atmosphere comes away a bit put out by the playing of rock music at maximum volume just above his head!

By far the most noticeable and effective thing we did was to lay a pale champagne-coloured carpet throughout the main state rooms and consign acres of particularly unappealing red plastic flooring to the dustbin. We were warned gloomily that pale colours would be catastrophic for large numbers of visitors. However, deeply impressed by the chic and persuasive young salesman in his wide-lapelled, double-breasted suit, I was deaf to reason, especially after he had allowed us to carry out market

*(left) Jon Culverhouse, House Manager*
*(right) Michael Scott, Agent*

research by putting a non-returnable sample of the said carpet in front of the sink where Harold stood to wash up, and we had seen that even after a week's hard labour it was still pristine. The salesman's advice that most dirt is pale coloured has stood the test of time; the carpet is now about ten years old and still looks marvellous.

All these early vital decorative decisions were taken with the essential help of Michael Scott, the agent on the estate. From the first day we arrived at Burghley he was a tower of strength. Most of the things we found so hard to cope with were decisions about management. My experience in the field was nearly nil, and it took a lot of getting used to. The business of doing up enormous rooms was also terrifying, and Michael patiently waited while I dithered about comparing colour samples and then, having reached a decision, had to be drip fed on gin until the room was complete and we could be sure a dreadful blunder had not been committed.

In order to tackle the furniture restoration we had to change things round in the state rooms. It drove our patient guides to despair; entering a room, they would announce, 'And here Ladies and Gentlemen ... No, it's not'. I found myself needing the services of restorers in every discipline, not just furniture, and all sorts of interesting people came on the scene at this time. There were over 600 paintings requiring attention and some were in a particularly parlous state. The trustees were very enthusiastic that we should start a rigorous programme of restoration all over the house and it is only a lack of funds which prevents us doing everything we want to do.

As well as embarking on the necessary restoration and decoration we had enormous fun prowling round the house wondering why my ancestors kept everything. The drawers of every cabinet and chest of drawers were stuffed, and every desk was a minefield of Victorian black-edged letters, mourning lockets with curls of hair inside, old gloves, broken chessmen, faded sepia photographs of nameless relations, pen wipers and so on. However, we made a discovery early on that taught us to be a little careful of what we discarded as rubbish.

Outside the door to Simon's dressing room stood a venerable black tin box – the sort that solicitors kept wills in, in the old days. We assumed that, like so many of its ilk, it would be crammed full of dreary Victorian screeds. Having barked his shins on it once too often, Simon decided it would have to go. We opened the lid and there, nestling on the top, were my father's fishing lures from his days as Governor of Bermuda, alarming confections of pink feathers with enormous hooks for catching blue marlin and sail fish. They were moth-eaten and past their best. Underneath were his bank statements for 1976. Right at the bottom was a letter signed by Elizabeth I, and two seventeenth-century deeds. An excellent lesson in not throwing away what you haven't looked at.

The 'Dark Nurseries' are Burghley's answer to attics: two huge rooms stacked floor to ceiling with a ravishing mixture of junk and treasures. They had no electricity when we came and were a fantastic hunting ground for the 'Look what I've found' game. Sadly, among the picturesque heaps were tragedies. Ten Venetian seventeenth-century walnut chairs, piled any-old-how had become a mass of broken and

*(opposite) One of the 'Dark Nurseries' in the days of clutter*

woodwormed limbs and bits. Beautiful gilded gesso mirrors with chairs and fire-irons tossed casually on top with the inevitable result that they were almost totally destroyed. Large paintings with smaller ones stacked confidentially against them, the frames nicely embedded in the canvas behind. And so it went on. Weeks and weeks of filthy, heavy labour to restore, for the first time for generations, order and clarity. Of course it is very boring now, all electrified and tidy, with no more discoveries to be made, – or are there? Time and time again this extraordinary house has given us surprises. Recently we had the thrill of the secret room ...

Ever since we attempted to get a grip on the house's historical past we have been assisted by the guiding hand of Dr Till. He was our GP when I lived here as a child, but all I can recall of his healing touch was a particularly nasty injection in my bottom for a boil. *Malgré tout* we have remained friends ever since. He is a brilliant historian and knows more about this house and its occupants than anyone. He has studied the generations of eccentric forebears and refers to them in conversation rather disconcertingly by their Christian names, 'poor John of course, he had terrible migraines'. Suddenly I am aware that he is referring to the seventeenth-century fifth Earl.

It was Dr Till who pointed out to us that the window underneath the clock tower did not quite tie up with the room inside. I recalled my aunt, Romayne Brassey, telling me of the time she and my father were soundly beaten for trying to find the 'secret room', also under the clock tower. The temptation was too much.

One Sunday morning a curious crowd gathered in the inner courtyard to gaze upwards where, outlined against the sky, a young Venture Scout was adjusting the harness around his middle. Urged on by his companions he carefully crept out along the narrow stone ledge with a drop below of about sixty feet. Inching round while we held our breath, he eventually gained the window ledge beneath the clock tower. Clinging by his finger tips he peered through the dusty window; 'What can you see?', 'A china

*(opposite) The Clock Tower and inner courtyard. The clock face is adorned with Lord Burghley's arms and the date 1585. It is possible that the three storeys below the clock were built earlier, with Flemish masonry carved by Henryk. The secret room is behind the two righthand panes of the oriel window on the third storey*

bowl,' he answered, 'What shall I do with it?' 'Break the window and bring it out' was our eager reply. I was already seeing headlines, 'Scout finds Japanese heirloom in Hidden Room'. Carefully he made a small hole in the leaded glass and withdrew a chipped tin-glazed pottery vessel with, astonishingly, a red substance inside smelling strongly of linseed oil. It turned out to be oil paint used to decorate one of the many painted rooms in the 1670s.

The little room under the tower had been sealed up when it was altered in 1674 to accommodate the curved walls necessary for decoration at that time, and beyond the partitions on both sides were apertures about three-feet wide, hardly deserving the title 'room' but big enough to leave a paint pot in for a few hundred years. We were just as excited about this discovery as if we had indeed found an heirloom.

Some discoveries seem amusing to the modern eye, though their original purpose was doubtless deeply worthy. Two splendid documents turned up when Felix Pryor was cataloguing the muniments room; they now grace our spare loo. The first was a receipt for twenty guineas given to qualify as a governor for life of the Magdalen Hospital for the Reception of Penitent Prostitutes by the tenth Earl of Exeter (1754–1804). The second is also a receipt for a donation of ten guineas by the tenth Earl, for a life subscription to The Society for the Relief of the Ruptured Poor. An impressive pair of gifts, except that they were probably designed to help him in his successful quest for a marquessate.

Not all discoveries are good news. Sometimes the smell of mildew in a cupboard heralds the most dread disease, dry rot. I was nearly eliminated by a plaster apple which fell from a seventeenth-century plaster-and-wood garland on the ceiling above my desk. This was an indication that the floor above needed to be taken up at once, before loads of tourists thundered through boards just about to give way. The trick is not to ignore warning signs when they occur and always to be prepared for disaster. It is someone's law that drains block on Christmas Day, that pipes burst at night and that down the back of every sofa is a honeymoon hotel and maternity unit for mice.

## EXHIBITIONS

BEFORE MY MOTHER'S DEATH, we had all been discussing the viability of an exhibition of the Burghley collection of Japanese and Chinese porcelain, properly researched and catalogued. She had been very keen on the idea and suddenly it seemed important, not just because she had wanted it to happen, but because we desperately needed something big to attract the press. The number of visitors had been dropping for some time and at the end of 1982 we were down to 49,000, our lowest annual total ever. The reason we chose to exhibit the oriental items was simple; we had an amazing story of discovery to tell which we hoped would attract the media and put Burghley more strongly back on the map as one of England's best-known houses.

Gordon Lang, a colleague from Sotheby's, came to have tea one day with Mama and me. Walking through the house for the first time he was struck by the quantity of oriental pieces of porcelain lying around. In particular, a beautiful and rare fifteenth-century Korean bottle with a metal mount round the neck caught his eye. He suggested the idea of an exhibition and a catalogue. After my mother died he came back to carry out the probate valuation and was even more amazed by the number of rare pots, dishes and animal figures he found in cupboards, almost all of them seventeenth-century Japanese.

I remember his coming to see me one morning and asking if we had any bills or inventories of the collection. Vaguely I recalled my father talking about the 1688 inventory. We went into the dusty, dark muniments room, where all the family manuscripts and letters are kept. In one of the heavy metal drawers was the old battered inventory, written in a clearly legible hand by Culpepper Tanner, the fifth Earl's secretary. On page fifty-two was the clear entry, 'Two China Boyes Wrestling'; it struck me like an electric shock. I knew immediately that they were the pair of wrestlers which, until a few years before, had been holding open the door of one of the State Rooms. This meant that this ancient volume was as current and useful as a reference book as it had ever been. A week or so later we knew we were sitting on the earliest inventoried collection of seventeenth-century Japanese porcelain in the world. I can never tell the story without a tingle running up my spine.

We collected all the oriental pieces we could relate to the inventory and placed them in the library on the ground floor, for ease of access. We

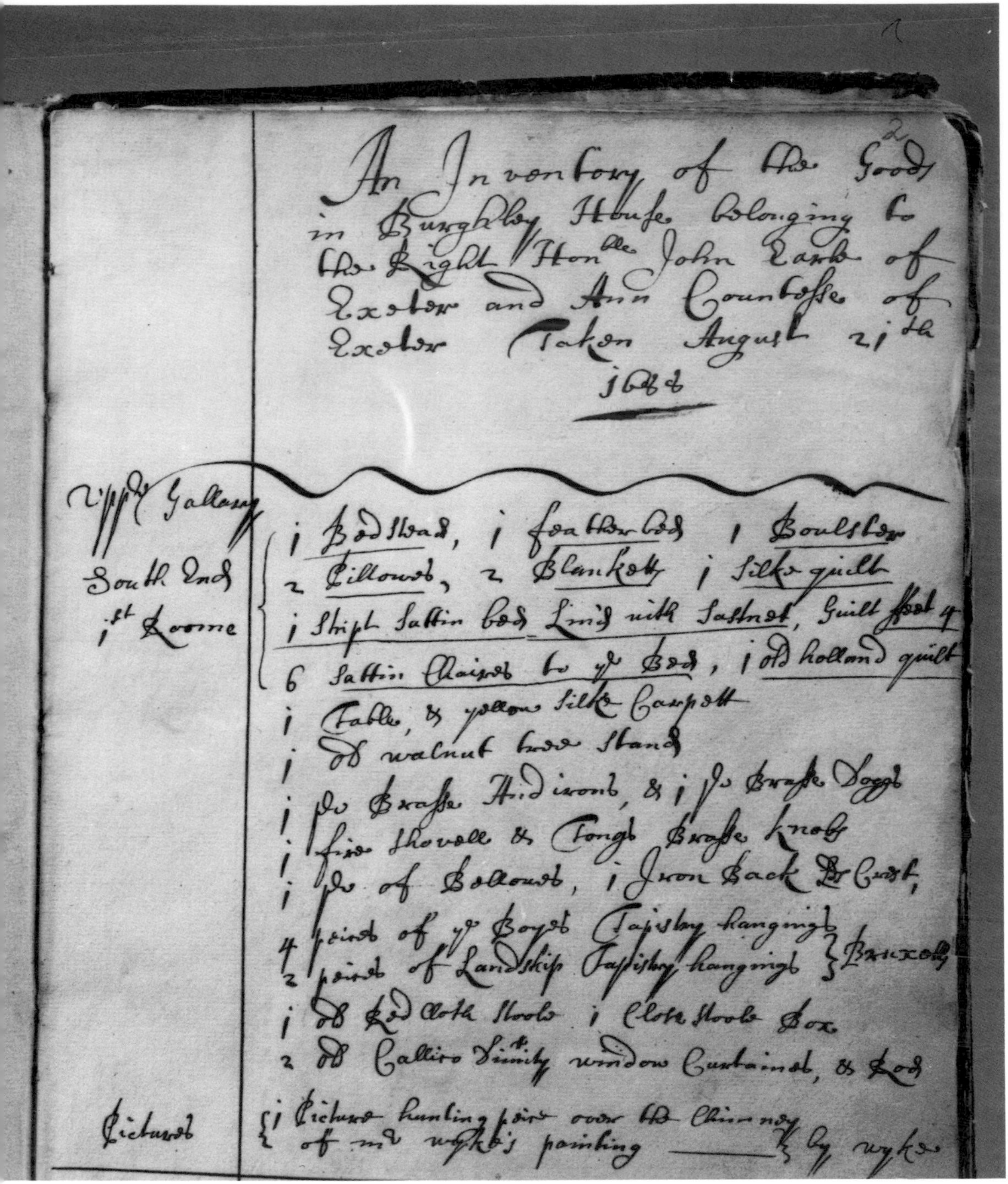

An Inventory of the Goods
in Burghley House belonging to
the Right Hon:ble John Earle of
Exeter and Ann Countesse of
Exeter Taken August 21:th
1688

Upper Gallery
South End
1st Roome

1 Bedstead, 1 feather bed, 1 Boulster
2 Pillowes, 2 Blankets, 1 Silke quilt
1 Strip't Sattin bed Lin'd with Sattnet, Quilt ffst 4
6 Sattin Chaires to y'e bed, 1 old holland quilt
1 Table, & yellow Silke Carpett
1 old walnut tree Stand
1 p'r Brasse Andirons, & 1 p'r brasse doggs
1 fire Shovell & Tongs brasse knobs
1 p'r of Bellowes, 1 Iron back & Crest,
4 peices of y'e Boyes Tapistry hanginge } Brussells
2 peices of Landskip Tapistry hanginge }
1 old Red Cloth Stoole 1 Close Stoole box
2 old Callico dimity window Curtaines, & Rods

Pictures
{ 1 Picture hunting peice over the Chimney
{ of m'r wykes painting ———— by wyke

*Title page of the 1688 inventory*

covered the table and overflowed onto the floor. A day later we nearly lost the lot. They were laying the new beautiful carpet in the State Rooms on the first floor. One of the men let a big roll of carpet fall from the vertical to the horizontal. It hit the floor with a great crash. Below was the library with a plaster ceiling decorated with roundels. One of these, about fourteen inches in diameter, was loosened by the impact and in turn fell, missing the heap of Ming blue-and-white porcelain on the table by a whisker. After this all the pots were put under the table; in order to catalogue them Gordon had to crawl.

Gordon stayed at Burghley before we moved in and after that came and set up camp in what became known as the 'Chapel Flat'. He diligently beavered away and gradually deciphered the ambiguous English of Mr Tanner. One of the puzzles was the description of a bowl as 'A Turkey colour Bowl'; what colour was 'Turkey', we wondered? A sort of grey with red wobbly bits under its beak? We searched for such a piece. No success. Then, while abluting in the bath one evening, it struck Gordon exactly what we were looking for – Turkey colour meant turquoise, Turkey coloured blue. Of course. We found the bowl without further trouble.

By sheer hard work Gordon got the catalogue off to the printers just in time. (I fell for the oldest ruse in the book – if you order more catalogues they get progressively cheaper per copy. We now insulate a loft with porcelain catalogues.) We all worked terribly hard to get the exhibition ready. The house was raided for display cupboards; anything with glass shelving was pressed into action. One cupboard proved too large for Steeles Removals to get upstairs into the exhibition room. The solution was simple; Mr Steele sawed it in half and then screwed it back together. The press party was at 12 noon and at 11.45 we were still labelling. Somehow, as the first journalistic footfall sounded on the stairs, it was done, the first of a continuing series of special exhibitions showing collections from the house. So far we have had one a year since 1983.

The press party was Sue Bond's idea. She had worked for many years in the Sotheby's press office and knew all the arts press well. She had just gone freelance when we moved to Burghley and suggested we could work together. I have never taken such a good decision as I did when I hired her expertise. She is enormously efficient, drives us all into the ground but gets very good results. We have a press day each year just before we open for the season, and this ensures good coverage for the forthcoming months.

That first party was a bit agonizing. I had no clue how to deal with members of the press. Some had come to see what sort of blunders we were making, some out of curiosity about how a woman was coping with the opening of a house full of decaying art, and yet more because of reports in the popular press that we had done down the other members of the family to get here in the first place and there was a family rift the size of the national debt. Fortunately those reports were not true – there were enough pressures without that – but the gossip columns were not helpful to our endeavours to pull the house round, and ill-informed rumours dogged the family for months.

In fact, the press day went off with a swing. Everyone seemed friendly and we had rave reviews about the exhibition in various publications. The following year it did not go quite so smoothly. There was a misunderstanding over the quantity of food we needed, and Harold, Sue Bond, Jon Culverhouse, our new administrator, and I, were to be seen frantically making tomato salads, prawn cocktails, in fact anything we could throw to the ravening hoards of press who were being stalled in the hall and given gallons of sherry to lull their hunger pangs. Finally we were ready but by then they were all so tiddly that I do not think much of any note was written.

The story of the Countess's gems was as exciting as that of the Japanese porcelain. In what has, since I have known it, been called 'Aladdin's Cave', in reality a large walk-in safe, we found mouldering trays full of sawdust. They were the type of wooden tray used by bakers and were piled one on top of the other. During the probate valuation they were passed by one expert to another with increasing excitement. Buried under the dusty layers were quantities of little, precious jewels and gems, small amber figures, enamelled caskets and book covers, buttons set with rubies, gold boxes and so on. At this point another inventory came to light. A little later than that of 1688, which had been so invaluable in our hunt for porcelain, this Deed of Gift written in flat format and dated 1690 was to fill equally vital gaps in our understanding of the house.

It was in fact the list of objects left to the wife of the seventeenth-century fifth Earl of Exeter by her mother, the Countess of Devonshire from Chatsworth. She had listed everything she was giving her daughter on her demise, because she did not trust her son-in-law. In addition, as this was long before the Married Women's Property Act, a woman could not leave items to whom she wished without legally registering the fact.

Among the things written on the Deed were lists of gems, precious stones, 'Agats', hardstones and gold objects. Here was our working document, just like the 1688 inventory, enabling us to identify these mysterious boxes of goodies.

A London antique dealer was recommended to us as a great expert on 'objets de vertu'. He was the most charming and urbane man and brought his wife here to lunch to inspect the recent find. We laid the little treasures out on the library table beside the 1690 Deed of Gift. After lunch we took the visitors through to inspect the collection, having made it clear that we would be honoured if he would write a catalogue to accompany an exhibition the following season.

His reaction was not, as we had hoped, ecstatic and enthusiastic. On the contrary, he gloomily surveyed the groaning table and said he was sorry to tell us this but, in his opinion, almost without exception the objects were fakes. The only half-decent thing on show was an eighteenth-century box by Neuber made from bloodstone and cornelian. We were appalled. Bang went our idea of an exhibition. What about the Deed of Gift? He shook his head, 'How do you know *that* is genuine?' We could not believe our ears. We were certain these things were those described in the Deed; if they were, then the expert was mistaken. How could they be fakes? The family might well have been short of cash but would never have bothered to get the things copied.

Much troubled and cast down we decided to try one more avenue. On the Monday morning following, I went with Simon on his early train to London, carrying with me two suitcases containing the treasures and the Deed of Gift. We did not speak much on the journey, for there was an enormous amount at stake and we were worried that the next year might be the first without an exhibition.

I took a taxi to the Victoria and Albert Museum. Climbing the stairs to the metalwork department I was much relieved to meet Anna Somers Cocks, whom I knew. Her particular expertise was in the field of seventeenth century, and earlier, works of art. We went into the office of another friend, Philippa Glanville, who specializes in silver. They watched in silence as I unpacked the cases. The silence lasted approximately three seconds. The office erupted. I was not allowed to finish unpacking. The room filled with people all talking at once and helping to unwrap. Then the Deed was spread out on the table. Anna looked at me, 'This is fantastic, an excellent seventeenth-century collection of Vertu, the only comparable one in this country was at Ham House. Do you realize that this must have a catalogue? What about an exhibition at Burghley?'

## SPONSORSHIP

T HE IDEA THAT WE COULD OBTAIN funding from commercial companies crept up on us slowly. The first time that we dared to ask for money for restoring objects in the house was when the Japanese and Chinese ceramics travelled to the USA in 1986, where they were exhibited at Japan House in New York and at the High Museum in Atlanta. American Express funded the whole enterprise and, in addition, we received a donation of £25,000 towards the cost of restoring books in the house.

It has always seemed perfectly logical to us to request a rental fee for objects loaned elsewhere. Traditionally, owners have taken the view that they were the lucky ones to have the honour of their possessions travelling abroad both for the greater glory of the house and the tricky invisible benefit of 'publicity'. In our view this is wrong. The items on loan run huge risks of damage due to changes in temperature and humidity, while the publicity gained is impossible to quantify and in any case is of limited duration. As a result of our first foray into the world of sponsorship the libraries at Burghley are now in a maintained and positive condition, something which seemed unlikely ever to happen. With reasonable financial returns, therefore, the risks of lending items for exhibition can be worth taking.

Sponsorship sometimes comes when you least expect it, and we have been very fortunate with the organizations we have dealt with. For the past few years the Three Day Event Horse Trials at Burghley have been sponsored by Remy Martin, known for their peerless cognac and ownership of the Krug and Piper Heidsieck champagne houses. Remy Martin is a family firm and the Heriard Dubreuils turned out to be a most charming and friendly group of individuals. Their generosity was even greater than we thought – in addition to the horse trials, they sponsored a bed!

The family came to dinner at Burghley in 1983 when Remy took over the sponsorship of the Trials. After dinner we walked round the state rooms and went through room after room which clearly showed signs of neglect and disrepair. In Queen Elizabeth's Bedroom the seventeenth-century bed hangings drooped sadly, the once rich brocade reduced to tatty shreds of dusty string, the fringing literally holding the curtains together. Silently the Dubreuils stood looking at the bed. Then Martine asked what would happen to the bed if it was not restored quickly. I had to tell her that because of lack of funds there was no chance of the bed being restored. It would continue to decay until the hangings disintegrated altogether. No more was said and we walked on round the rooms.

Two weeks later I received a curious telegram: 'We spoke about beds after dinner ... Please come to London to discuss this.' Sitting at lunch in a staid London club, Ralph Browning, senior executive of Remy's marketing company, turned to me and uttered the magical words, 'Remy Martin would like to underwrite the cost of refurbishing the State Bed. How much will it cost?' Hopeless with figures, I calculated in biro on the palm of my hand so many metres at so much and unfortunately came to a totally wrong conclusion, for while adding up I lost a nought. How cheap, we thought, how reasonable. Much to my embarrassment, the horrible true figure then emerged – £32,000. Would any company, even one as generous as Remy Martin, see this as a good investment? We did not know how the family in Cognac would react, nor did Ralph. We went home gloomily convinced that the funds would not appear. A month later a letter came: 'Dear Victoria, please commence restoration.'

The commercial bandwagon had started to roll and the bed would be ready for the new season. Eugene Shortall, an inspired interior designer, began researching beds and hangings at the Victoria and Albert Museum with the help of Sheila Landi from the textile conservation department. A design was arrived at, and a fabric, made and dyed by Richard Humphries in Suffolk, was chosen. It was a moreen, a woollen material with a silky watermark, very right for the period and dyed to a misty blue green. It looked just the thing.

The next stage was the couched thread embroidery which was done in Paris, perhaps at the very workshops where the original bedspread was made in the seventeenth century. The old trimmings and passementerie were cleaned and replaced and, one freezing day, Sheila and her colleagues began to re-assemble the bed. Looking at it today, no one could imagine the effort and excitement that went into the production of such a masterpiece. All I know now is that it has become a star instead of an embarrassment, and the guides were so overcome that for a good while it became the 'Remy Martin Bed' – a little puzzling to academic historians visiting the house.

Since the days of the Remy Martin gift, we have had the good fortune to have another bed restored by a local charitable trust; and Seibu, the Japanese department store group, paid for the Marquetry Room to be totally redecorated, and underwrote the cost of cleaning the large Mattia Preti painting in the Ante-Chapel, in return for a loan exhibition of assorted works of art from the house. Mr Higashi, the manager with whom we dealt was a model sponsor. When I asked him how he would like us to spend the sponsorship funding, he thought for a moment and then replied, 'Cleaning of a picture'. 'What sort of picture would you like to clean, Mr Higashi?'. More heavy thought, then a wide smile: 'A big one' came the answer.

The wonderful Paolo Veronese altarpiece in the Chapel has been conserved thanks to Sotheby's, and the Jewel Closet rehung with silk paid for by Berwin la Roche (a London financial advice company). The story continues. More recently, a Stamford company, Newage International, has sponsored the restoration of two pieces of furniture. In all cases the money has been spent on projects chosen by the companies concerned, safe in the knowledge that we would not contemplate selling the restored items, and in return we have tried to contribute something of worth to the donor company. This would be the loan of items for an exhibition, publicity, a location for corporate entertaining or whatever seemed sensible to them. These days 'heritage' is a valuable tool for the image makers and can benefit businesses in many different ways.

# CHAPTER THREE

# THE ANCESTORS

I N MOST FAMILY HISTORIES there are those who stand out. Where there is a great house it is ancestors who collect, buy land, marry heiresses or commit some appalling crime, such as allowing the house to burn down or gambling away the estate, whose names are remembered. Among the Cecils, Sir William Cecil, who built the house, is obviously important.

## THE BUILDER

SIR WILLIAM CECIL, the first Lord Burghley (1520–98), was the pre-eminent statesman of the Elizabethan age, serving the Virgin Queen for forty years.

Cecil was educated at St John's College, Cambridge, from which he graduated in 'logick' at the age of fourteen, and was destined to become a lawyer. He had an excellent command of Greek and Latin and this, coupled with an introduction from his father, earned him a place at Court working in a lowly capacity for Henry VIII. During the reign of Edward VI, Cecil worked as Secretary to Protector Somerset, but when Mary ascended the throne in 1553 he retired from Court, although it is thought that she offered him a position in spite of his Anglicanism. When Elizabeth succeeded Mary in 1558 Cecil was well placed to take the position of Secretary of State and subsequently became Lord High Treasurer.

His capacity for hard work, his organizational skills, attention to detail and incorruptibility made him a valued servant and he was as loyal and honest to his fiery-tempered employer as it was possible to be. Cecil was an astute thinker and the Queen was able to rely on his judgement and counsel absolutely. She once said that 'No prince in Europe hath such a counsellor as I have in mine'. His was the guiding hand behind the policies which made Elizabeth's reign so notable.

Domestic and foreign policy were inextricably entwined; it was essential for Lord Burghley (he was ennobled in 1571) to be aware of the intrigues and plots originating on the Continent as well as of events so far afield as Russia and the Americas. He was probably one of the most accomplished spy-masters ever to have operated on England's behalf. Here at Burghley we have his working atlas, a wonderful testament to his interest in foreign affairs. Printed by Ortelius in Antwerp in 1574, it was coloured by his sister and sold in several parts – a cunning ruse followed much later by, among others, Chippendale, with his 'Director'. Essentially you had to go on buying month after month or else you ended up with an atlas which only contained Asia. Pretty useless. Lord Burghley's atlas contains such vital information as: 'The safe houses in France where an English emissary might stay safely' and 'A full list of the Czar of All The Russias' titles'. There is also a note of Frobisher setting off on a maraud, as well as how the winds behave at a certain time of the year on the route to America.

Lord Burghley was both cautious and mercenary, on his own account and that of the nation. He favoured financial gambles taken on behalf of the Queen by her acquisitive sailors, but remained carefully in the background. That way he would not be accused of making financial gains from their piratical escapades, and at the same time minimized his own risk if they were to founder.

As for his personal affairs, why did Lord Burghley choose to build a 'prodigy' house in Lincolnshire?[*] By anybody's estimate it was not a fashionable part of the world. The explanation is, of course, that he was enlarging an existing family property, inherited from his father in 1552 and still lived in by his mother. It is possible that the Cecil home comprised the remains of St Michael's Priory, closed by Henry VIII. There was a sister house to this institution up the hill at Wothorpe: a nunnery where the Abbess was fired for 'undue levity of spirit'.

Construction of the house extended over thirty-two years. State papers reveal that the east range was being built in 1555 and the north front was completed in 1587. Some genius put a great deal of thought into the exact positioning of the house and that of the drains. Someone once told me, 'If you want to get off on the right foot with a duke, discuss drains'.

[*] The term 'prodigy' meaning 'exceptional, enormous' is used to describe houses of this period, such as Burghley, Longleat and Hardwick Hall.

*Roof of the north range looking west. The chimneys are disguised as Doric columns (Country Life)*

Be that as it may, the drains here all empty into a natural fault in the limestone, ending up, as far as we know, just about level with the main Leicester to Peterborough railway line. To date there has never been the slightest bother with this natural drainage, only of course from time to time with the drain pipes which block at crucial moments, adding to the air of frenzied jollity on a warm summer bank holiday.

In the period Burghley was being built it was not the custom to employ an architect. Most of the design for the superlative roof and idosyncratic clock tower was, therefore, probably the work of the owner. He was certainly in touch with Sir John Thynne, who had just completed Longleat, and the names of artisans were sent to Cecil. There has been much discussion about the origin of these roof elements – were they inspired by buildings in the Middle East or by the palaces being built in France and Italy? We do not know for sure. But the roof at Burghley is

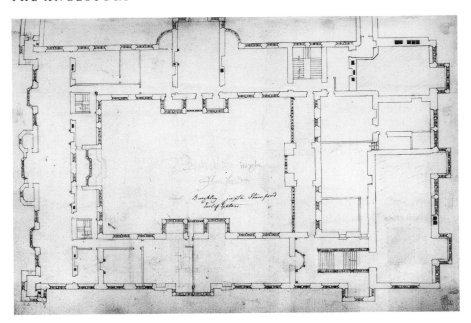

*Plan of the first floor c.1600 by John Thorpe, just after completion of the house. Note the long gallery on the west side (Sir John Soane's Museum)*

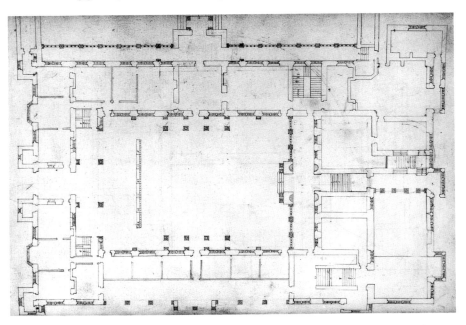

*Plan of the ground floor c.1600 by John Thorpe, just after completion of the house. Note the open loggia on the south front, closed in by the 5th Earl (Sir John Soane's Museum)*

74

probably the finest in England, although run a close second by that of Longleat. Both have turrets and so-called 'Banketting houses' – dry and private rooms ideal for romantic dalliance or political intrigue. It is a recognized fact that one of the reasons for Elizabethan houses having such complicated roofs is because they were used for recreation by their owners. Up on the roof you escaped the vile smells of rudimentary plumbing, the chatter of the servants and the ever possible danger in those days of being overheard by someone who did not hold your interests dear to his bosom.

The roof is mostly covered with lead, laid over timber. There are also areas of a local stone known as Collyweston slate. This was mined in the village of Collyweston until the middle of this century, dug out from sandy mines about sixty feet below ground. The chunks of stone came to the surface in blocks called 'logs', which were sprayed with water and the frost allowed to get into them. They then split naturally into slates. No slates have been made in this way for some time and their price has gone up to dizzy heights, no pun intended.

The windows were originally diamond paned load lights, and the façade of the house was quite flat. As a rule, the windows of sixteenth-century houses are not recessed as in eighteenth-century examples and have shallow window sills. The house must have appeared a little austere and bleak in those early days. The inner court, around which the house is built, had at this time superb proportions, sadly lost when, in 1828, the arcaded ground floor corridors were enclosed and a passage built above them. How on earth the inhabitants lived here with them open, defies imagination, but the proportions no doubt cheered them greatly as they sped round trying to avoid hypothermia.

The old kitchen is the only vaguely Elizabethan room remaining. What a shame that the fifth Earl did such a thorough job in the seventeenth century; it would have been good to have had just one original panelled room with a marvellous oak bed. The house must have been dreadfully uncomfortable in those early days of the 1570s and 1580s. Draughty, underfurnished and no doubt dark and gloomy too. While the building was in progress, Lord Burghley kept an eye on events from London, but when he did come up it was by a somewhat peculiar means of locomotion – he rode here on a donkey. It took about four days and was easier on his chronic gout than gallivanting about on a restive horse. Perhaps it also gave him a chance to look at the southern part of his estate. It certainly is always good for a chuckle when I give lectures in America to announce as a caption to a slide, 'And here is the first Lord Burghley on his ass'.

Farmland surrounds Burghley; it is the central point of the estate. Lord Burghley would, presumably, meet his steward and discuss crops, yields, sheep and so forth, when he came, but it is doubtful whether he ever lived in the house for any length of time. He was building it for

*Lord Burghley on his ass (Ashmolean Museum, Oxford)*

future generations of his family; one of the best reasons for building after all. It has retained this family atmosphere throughout the generations, and visitors often comment on it.

As far as we know, Lord Burghley did not use the house for Court entertaining. It makes one wonder what exactly he envisaged for those huge spaces such as the great hall and his long galleries on the south and west. I have this rather absurd vision of etiolated ladies, seldom exposed to fresh air, ploughing up and down the galleries for exercise, in their great dresses: 'One hundred and one, one hundred and two' etc. Rather like doing lengths at the swimming baths today.

Lord Burghley spent most of his time at Theobalds near Cheshunt (now destroyed) and two other Cecil houses – in the Strand and at Wimbledon. He entertained the Queen at Theobalds on a number of occasions and it was there that he installed his renowned system for feeding travellers. Whether they were known to him or not, a repast was available at his table for gentlemen who cared to call. Those who were of more humble estate were also catered for and their horses fed and watered while they ate.

As Lord Burghley grew old, he must have despaired for the future of his great house once it fell into the careless hands of 'my bad son Thomas', his heir and successor. The old man's culture was prodigious: he collected marble Caesars' heads before Lord Arundel made such antiquarian taste popular, his library was famous all over England and he built up a fine collection of pictures, coins, gems, and gold and silver plate. This discriminating taste was not evident in the rather raffish and military elder son. With his prolonged periods of absence on soldierly duty, who was going to manage the house?

It was often the case with historic houses that the owners' wives rescued them from the neglect or misuse of their husbands and kept them going. This happened in various ways, either by dint of handsome jointures or, as in the case of Thomas's wife Dorothy Nevill, an estate in Yorkshire at Snape, near Bedale. The Cecils kept Snape and lived there off and on in the castle. Dorothy was presumably capable and up to the task of managing two such large enterprises.

Lord Burghley had another son, as well as two daughters, by his second marriage (his first wife, Thomas's mother, died) to Mildred Cooke. It was this son, Robert Cecil, later Lord Salisbury, who stepped into his father's professional shoes and coped with the aged Queen, bereft after the death of Lord Burghley, and her successor, James I. It was Robert Cecil who acquired Hatfield House, where his descendants have lived ever since, in a direct house-swap with the King for Theobalds.

## THOMAS, 1ST EARL OF EXETER (1542–1622)

THOMAS, ELDER SON of the Lord Treasurer, never fulfilled his father's wishes for him to be a studious, diplomatic successor at court. He was not at all interested in courtly life, but he was a brave and talented soldier. In 1574 he had fought under the Earl of Murray as part of the force trying to free Edinburgh castle, which had been taken over by Scottish rebels. He also fought in Flanders at Zutphen in 1586 (the same battle where the poet Sir Philip Sidney was fatally wounded) and was a volunteer on board a ship of the British Fleet when the Spanish Armada attacked in 1588. When the Queen's favourite, Lord Essex, headed an insurrection in 1601 Thomas put it down, and was very nearly shot in the process, but was rewarded by being made a Knight of the Garter.

When his father died in 1598 Thomas was the chief mourner at the funeral and was instructed by the Queen to mourn 'as an Earl'. But he turned down such a preferment from the Queen because he could not afford the expense that the lifestyle of an earl would demand; by his own reckoning he was very poor indeed.

The Queen died in 1603. Thomas and his half-brother Robert were created earls on the same day by King James I in 1605: Robert as Earl of Salisbury in the morning, and Thomas as Earl of Exeter after lunch. The family had no connection with Exeter, it was simply a title that was free because the previous holder had been attainted for treason. Thomas had earned the title by serving Elizabeth and James well. Perhaps his financial situation had improved, or else it was a matter of keeping up with the Salisburys. Nonetheless, the fact that he built the large secondary house of Wothorpe, near Stamford, seems at odds with a man suffering from a cash crisis. Perhaps it was a case of 'the pleasure remembered long after the price is forgotten'. The house was later destroyed because the family could not afford the upkeep of two great houses (and the water system at Wothorpe gave people cholera and typhoid), and it was this building which furnished Capability Brown with stone for the stables at Burghley; it has been a ruin ever since. In addition, the Earl had inherited

Wimbledon Manor and used it to entertain the Queen.

The new King, James I, was invited to stay at Burghley by Thomas, one of the first English peers to ask the King to his home. In fact the monarch stayed at Burghley twice because, following the visit to the house, he fell off his horse on the road north and was brought back to the house badly bruised and shaken. He was cared for at Burghley until he could ride again.

Thomas died in 1622 aged eighty-one. He was much admired for his successful military career and his service and friendship to Queen Elizabeth in her old age and to King James I but, rather unfairly, has been unappreciated by his descendants. I suspect he would be considered rather a success if he had been the son of anyone else. He was certainly distinguished enough to gain an Earldom through his own endeavours and his lack of bookishness did him no harm in the long run.

## WILLIAM, 2ND EARL (1566–1640)

WHEN WILLIAM WAS A BOY he was taken to Europe by Mr Bird, his tutor, and found that there were certain advantages to being the grandson of the Treasurer. He was sumptuously housed by Cardinal Farnese in Italy, with five menservants to wait on him.

William was knighted by James I and together with his cousin Lord Cranborne, carried the King's train in procession at Westminster at the celebrations to acknowledge the Crown Prince. When this same prince died in 1612 Sir William Cecil was a pall bearer. He was obviously rather good at carrying things ... And he was called on to assist at another funeral in 1625, three years after he had become the second Earl at the age of 56, that of King James. The Earl was made a Privy Councillor in 1625 and in 1630 installed as a Knight of the Garter. He does not appear to have lived much at Burghley, preferring to be in his house in London, near the centre of political life.

The Earl's first wife, the daughter of the Earl of Rutland, died young but having given him a son. She was a baroness in her own right so her son inherited this title and became Lord Roos. The young lord was taken to Italy with his tutor, John Molle, who had the misfortune to be clapped in irons by the Inquisition and died, still a prisoner, thirty years later. Lord Roos himself fared little better: he was poisoned in the suburbs of

Naples in 1618. As a result the title of Earl of Exeter passed to the Earl's nephew because his second marriage produced three daughters and no son.

## DAVID, 3RD EARL (d.1643)

THE THIRD EARL ONLY HELD the title for three years (1640–3). He was very good at begetting children, he and his wife producing six sons and three daughters, but only two survived.

## JOHN, 4TH EARL (1628–78)

THE FOURTH EARL WAS ONLY fifteen when he inherited the title from his father. Living at Burghley with his mother and grandmother must have been rather boring, but on 23 July 1643 matters livened up somewhat when Oliver Cromwell and a considerable number of soldiers drove a party of Royalists, under the command of Lord Camden, from Stamford to Burghley and laid siege to them at the house.

Lord Camden was a cousin to the young earl and family loyalty would have governed the welcome he was given, but in the rather testing circumstances I wonder how pleased the two old ladies and young boy were to see the courtyards full of noisy cursing soldiers, sweating horses, wounded men, and across the stream at the bottom of the garden the menacing sight of ordnance massing on the hill under the command of Cromwell himself.

It was not Cromwell's desire to storm a house containing old women and children, but he did want to have Lord Camden. This rather dashing young Catholic nobleman had been a thorn in his flesh for a long time and had caused him to lose many men. He had even raised a local force called the Camdeners, who had tangled with the Puritan regiments and caused havoc among the local people in their search for food and lodgings.

An offer to parley came from Cromwell's parliamentary troops. From the roof of the house Lord Camden would have seen the opposite hill

*(opposite) The 1st Earl of Exeter, English School c.1610*

*The south front which*
*Cromwell assaulted in 1643*
*(Country Life)*

*The 4th Earl*

crawling with troops. He was hopelessly outnumbered with only 200 men, but he refused the offer. As night fell the inhabitants of the house must have feared for their lives. Burghley was vulnerable; easily approached on all four sides, its two great cannon, relics from the Armada campaign, were on the wrong side of the house, virtually immobile and had no ammunition. The talking must have gone on all night in the smoky dining room. Perhaps the household spent the hours of darkness packing away the most treasured objects and paintings for storage in the cellar. The housemaids were probably all of a twitter, and the indignation of the two old ladies at the rude interruption to their daily affairs must have been considerable.

At first light on July 24 the bombardment by the Parliamentary troops began. The cannon balls whizzed across the water, striking the stone wall with a great thud and raising clouds of dust as the limestone shattered. Broken glass lay on the paving slabs round the house and the smoke from the ordnance rose into the still summer morning.

Lord Camden had no death wish for himself, nor did he wish to see his cousin's great palace wrecked. He and his troops withstood the barrage for a few hours and then agreed to surrender. They were taken prisoner and marched away with no lives lost. It is believed that Cromwell, having achieved his military aim, then graciously invited himself to stay for a few weeks, although maybe a judicious welcome was offered by the old ladies and the young lord. As a token of his good wishes he presented the family with a portrait of himself by Walker, which now, ironically, hangs opposite the one of Charles I. When one of the two pictures needed cleaning, I believe it was Cromwell's, we diplomatically had them done together. We are not Lord Burghley's descendants for nothing!

## JOHN, 5TH EARL (1648–1700)

THE FOUR GENERATIONS of Cecils after Lord Burghley did nothing of note to the house, but in the late seventeenth century the reign of the fifth Earl and Countess transformed and embellished the house almost beyond recognition.

John Exeter's considerable taste was greatly aided because he did the sensible thing and married a considerable heiress, Anne Cavendish,

*The 5th Earl of Exeter by Godfrey Kneller*

*Anne, wife of the 5th Earl, by Godfrey Kneller*

daughter of the third Earl of Devonshire. She was already a widow when they married. Her first husband, Lord Rich, had lived up to his name and she came to Burghley as a wealthy young woman. It was certainly a love match. The couple shared a passion for beautiful objects and a lust for adventure and foreign travel. They indulged both fancies by travelling to Europe at least four times. On the first visit in 1679 their entourage included their young son, a tutor, a chaplain, a secretary, various women and menservants, soldiers, large numbers of horses, camping equipment, the family coach and a small dog called Towser.

The first problem that arose came from the introduction of the men-at-arms to French ale houses. It resulted in gaggles of intoxicated soldiery having to be left behind, to catch up with the cavalcade as best they might as it moved ponderously on towards Italy. The horses reacted badly to the increase in temperature and unaccustomed forage, and the cure seems to have involved washing them in wine – which does not speak well for that particular vintage.

No one had warned the Exeters that the weather was a trifle hotter in Siena than Stamford in July. They had gone prepared with all their finery, velvet cloaks, warm worsted breeches and so on. These were sold by the side of the road in an early version of the car-boot sale. Guns proved to be a mixed blessing. Firstly, all the men who were needed to fire and maintain them were still lurching about in France. Secondly, when a weapon was taken into an Italian walled city, a large fine was payable. Soon the guns (short-barrelled muskets referred to as 'Kerbens'), unsold clothes and unused camping equipment were packed up in a large crate and returned to Burghley.

The Earl and Countess were learning rapidly how to adapt to foreign travel. Even the splendid Culpepper Tanner, the Earl's secretary, while recording their journey and purchases as they bumpily progressed south, began to write in Italian of a sort: 'Una notte per 5 cavalli ...', 'due a cena servitori per tre giorni ...' He describes buying ice creams: 'A large one for My Lord, one smaller for myself.' The Countess was carried on a litter over rough terrain, although it seems that the person really in need of tender treatment was Culpepper; he contracted pleurisy and pneumonia along the way and nearly died. He records purchases of everything from paintings to 'Balsam Apoplecticum' (Friars' Balsam I presume), including all sorts of tourist trivia: 'Venice Treacle', 'sprigs of jewellery', 'Ye medal of Ye Pope', 'A Daphne and Apollo in ivory'.

The paying for and packing of all these items was left to poor Tanner, who frequently remained behind the main party to settle up and arrange the shipping of goods to England. In this he was assisted by various agents who were used to the iniquitous ways of the customs and who would expedite matters. A man called John Hobson and the Consul in Venice were sources of advice and a Mr Balle of Genoa was another. Tanner also described business carried out with 'A low creeping fellow, one Simon', who bought some of the discarded second-hand items when the family left Florence.

The cavalcade eventually arrived in Florence at the court of Cosimo de' Medici, Grand Duke of Tuscany. The Exeters did not actually stay with him but with a luckless fellow called Count Lorenzini whose job it was to entertain the growing number of aristocratic tourists turning up on the doorstep. Count Lorenzini was feeling a little bruised by a recent encounter with an unsatisfactory house guest – My Lord Winchester, who committed one blunder after another, firstly travelling without a chaplain and secondly being permanently drunk. After him the cultured Earl and his young wife were an instant success.

Very soon John Exeter and the Grand Duke were off buying paintings together. Artists were often commissioned to paint two versions of the same subject; I wonder if there was a bulk discount? The interesting thing about their purchases is that the artists were mostly still living, the fashion for buying antique works of art having not yet arrived. We can only guess at the impact the 'modern' mythical and religious pictures must have made on visitors when they arrived back at Burghley. However, we do know from Celia Fiennes's diary that when she was shown round the house by the housekeeper, she was shocked at the number of pictures featuring naked women which hung in the Earl's bedroom. Piety was no excuse for nudity it seems.

This first trip took two years in all, ending with a visit to Paris. There the Earl bought furniture, and tapestries from Monsieur Jans at the Gobelins factory. The tapestries at Burghley are superb, and when one considers the complications of measuring the walls, and making sure that the hangings were exactly right for the spaces allotted them, the outcome is quite impressive.

The fifth Earl, being a modern man, and having seen how comfortable the Italians were in their huge *palazzi*, was no longer prepared to live in a draughty, dirty, old-fashioned, inconvenient Elizabethan house. He

*The Burghley Bowl. This 18th-century Chinese export bowl (c.1738) shows the south front as it was in 1754 when the 9th Earl inherited the title, and prior to the refenestration and levelling of the skyline carried out by Capability Brown*

*(opposite) Brownlow, 9th Earl of Exeter, in Vandyke costume by Thomas Hudson*

swept away the long galleries on the first floor on the west and south fronts, replacing them with interconnecting rooms, and on the ground floor created matching apartments for himself and his wife. The extra wall space thus gained was used to hang his new collection of over 300 paintings.

The family gradually expanded with the arrival of several more children. There were also three more marauds across the Channel to buy works of art. While they were abroad the house was constantly being worked on by the two leading decorative painters of the day: Antonio Verrio and Louis Laguerre. The celebrated ironworker, Jean Tijou, was responsible for the finely crafted gilded gates on the west front. No doubt many other carvers, gilders, locksmiths, marquetry workers and so on were also exercising their talents. It would have been most uncomfortable to remain at home with this much work in progress. We can only rejoice that the Earl and Countess occupied themselves so profitably, if not for their bank balances, then for the good of the house.

The articles which the Earl chose for the house demonstrate that here was a man who bought with a real eye for quality. The cabinet on stand by King Louis XIV's supplier, Pierre Gôle, for example, is a dazzling item and so is the more restrained pewter boulle table made by Gerrit Jensen. The couple's picture-buying spree created the greatest collection of baroque Italian pictures in a British private house.

Both John and Anne did, however, die hugely in debt, over £8,000 each. John died at Issy just outside Paris in 1700 from, it was reported, 'a surfeit of fruit'. His widow returned to Burghley and continued to embellish the house, the final triumph being an enormous and splendid marble monument to them both made by a sculptor called Monnot. It is in the family chapel of St Martin's Church in Stamford, opposite the Tudor effigies of the Treasurer and his parents.

## JOHN, 6TH EARL (1674–1721)

LITTLE IS KNOWN ABOUT this Earl although it might be suspected that he spent his whole life worrying about the enormous debts left behind by his father. He married twice, the first time for less than a year and his wife died without issue, the second time to Elizabeth Brownlow of Belton House, who bore him five sons and one daughter.

*(left) The 6th Earl, (centre) The 7th Earl, (right) The 8th Earl*

## JOHN, 7TH EARL (1700–22)

SON OF THE SIXTH EARL, the seventh Earl died, unmarried, a few months after succeeding to the title.

## BROWNLOW, 8TH EARL (1701–54)

BROTHER OF THE SEVENTH EARL, Brownlow married a considerable heiress, Hannah-Sophia Chambers, to whom we are indebted for the existence of the enormous silver wine cooler in the Great Hall. It had been ordered by the fifth Earl but it could not be paid for until Hannah-Sophia's father, delighted with his daughter's marriage into the aristocracy, settled the account.

*Henry, 10th Earl and 1st Marquess of Exeter*

*(opposite) The 10th Earl (later 1st Marquess), his wife Sarah Hoggins (the 'Cottage Countess'), and their daughter Sophia, by Thomas Lawrence*

## BROWNLOW, 9TH EARL (1725–93)

AFTER THE TREASURER and the fifth Earl, the ninth Earl is the third major figure in the history of the house. Succeeding to the title in 1754, at the age of twenty-nine, he spent nearly forty years embellishing Burghley. Under the Earl's supervision Capability Brown was employed at Burghley from 1756 to 1779, making changes inside the house and out (particularly, levelling the skyline of the south front between the angle turrets, and removing the low northwest wing to improve the view of the house), and landscaping the park.

The Earl appears to have regarded it as his duty to complete the rooms unfinished by the fifth Earl, and he collected pictures which he felt were in the same idiom. He obviously derived enormous pleasure from interior decoration and good furniture, and was meticulous in his choice of craftsmen. He patronized Angelica Kauffman, Ince and Mayhew, and Newton and Fell. John Linnell, who is better known as a cabinet maker, was employed here in the 1770s, to add carved decoration to the George Rooms.

The Earl made four journeys to Italy and was recorded buying paintings in Rome and Naples, dining with the actor and dramatist, David Garrick, and with Mr Byers and Mr Jenkins, both well-known figures on the dilletante scene. It is also rumoured that he obtained the beautiful Francesco Bassano, *Adoration of the Magi* (now in the Red Drawing Room), in Venice, transporting it 'by night in a gondola'.

The Earl was a complicated man, prone to make extensive lists about everything from the recipe for a tar wash for fruit trees, to a cure for the smallpox. Terrified of being buried alive, he specifically asked that his coffin should not be nailed down until he started to 'show signs of mortification'.

## HENRY, 10TH EARL AND 1ST MARQUESS OF EXETER (1754–1804)

THE STORY OF THE TENTH EARL is almost beyond belief; in fact, until they lapsed, the film rights to the tale were held by the producer son of Donald Sinden.

In middle age the ninth Earl of Exeter realized that in spite of being married twice (his first wife died young) he was unlikely to have any children. He began to cast about in his mind as to whom he should choose as his heir. His closest male relation was Thomas Chambers Cecil, an alcoholic brother who had fled to France to avoid debtors and scandal in equal measure. While there, he had really made sure of his popularity at home by taking up with a Basque actress, Charlotte Gornier, who is said to have played Columbine on the Paris stage to rave reviews.

Thomas had political aspirations and was constantly begging the ninth Earl to bail him out of his financial trouble so that he could return to England and stand as a member of parliament. One of his letters asking for funds begins: 'My dear Friend and Brother, I would have replied to your kind and generous letter sooner but for my illness which has affected my nerves making it impossible to hold a pen as my hand shakes so. This very morning when I arose, I was bright yellow with the jaunders [sic], like a lemon from my head to my feet, I cannot imagine what has precipitated this attack.'

The Earl was at his wits' end as to how to keep his brother out of trouble, and hopefully curb his drinking. In the end he sent the prim and proper Miss Sutton, who acted as half nurse and half companion and who stayed with Thomas and Charlotte until Thomas died of an 'apoplectick fit'. He was interred beneath a blue stone at the parish church of St Michel de Gastel, near Bois-le-Duc. Charlotte was left penniless and wrote to the Earl asking for money to live on. History does not relate whether he heeded her plea.

Thomas's and Charlotte's son, Henry, had been brought over to England as a very small boy and brought up by the ninth Earl at Burghley. Thomas agreed to this because he thought that when his son was tenth Earl he would assist Thomas's political ambitions. Henry regarded his uncle as his father. There was a good deal of affection between them; he is referred to in letters as 'Harry', and there is a charming quote in which the Earl says 'God knows I love that boy, nor could I love him more were he indeed my own son.'

When Henry was old enough to consider matrimony, his father was more than interested. Thomas hoped for a good match to an heiress so that he could then play on filial loyalty, come back to England and live off the young couple. However, when the ninth Earl planned an extended trip to Europe following the death of his first wife, he left strict instructions that 'If Mr Cecil, taking advantage of my absence abroad should come to Burghley, Mr Hurst [steward] may inform him if he stays there or in this

*Isabella Poyntz, wife of the 2nd Marquess, by Thomas Lawrence*

neighbourhood for one day, my yearly allowance of 200 pounds ... shall be withdrawn the moment I hear of it.'

In due course a marriage was contracted between Miss Emma Vernon and Mr Henry Cecil. In spite of the machinations of Henry's unsatisfactory father, all should have been rosy for the young couple. No doubt Emma brought a ray of sunshine into the masculine lifestyle at Burghley. However, matters did not continue so happily and Emma fell in love with a consumptive curate, the Revd Sneyd, driven from her husband by his unacceptable monetary extravagances and because he was, quite possibly, spoilt and immature. Caught in a compromising situation by her husband, there was nothing for it but flight. She left home with the parson, leaving Henry alone and mortified by the whole business. Simultaneously, he was being dunned by creditors and living way above the allowance given him by the Earl, much to that gentleman's irritation.

Feeling, perhaps, that Emma had only married him for his title and potential wealth, Henry disguised himself as a humble painter, took the name of John Jones (which also had the effect of losing his debtors), and went to Shropshire. There in the small hamlet called Great Bolas, where there was a family property, he lodged with the local cow doctor, a Mr Hoggins

Henry very much enjoyed his double life. He went to enormous lengths to disguise himself and his whereabouts from those to whom he was in debt and also, perhaps, his uncle. In March 1790 Henry's letters to his lawyer tell of a new interest. Mr Hoggins was possessed of a beautiful young daughter Sarah, and it was she who captivated Henry now. Events took their course and the couple fell in love. However, not only did they fall in love but, rather absent mindedly given that he was still married to Emma Vernon, Henry married Miss Hoggins. As far as his young bride knew he was John Jones a landscape painter.

We cannot be certain when Henry told Sarah (the so-called 'Cottage Countess') who he really was. She must have been a trifle perplexed by the messengers who arrived for her husband. His clothes and possessions were above average for an artisan. Happily adoring however, she did not doubt him for an instant and maybe it was not until the old Earl of Exeter asked to meet Sarah, after the couple were married in 1791, that she became aware of the whole picture. Can you imagine how she must have felt, approaching the enormous house for the first time? And then servants hurrying forward out of the shadows to call her 'My Lady',

bobbing curtsies and laying out her simple country gowns from Great
Bolas.

As it happened, the ninth Earl was much taken with Sarah. He
learned that she was very fond of Parmesan cheese and sent her some as a
gift upon their return to Shropshire. For the time being he agreed to keep
Henry's address secret, rather supporting the theory that it was creditors
he was hiding from. Following a divorce discreetly managed later in 1791
another marriage took place, this time in the Church of St Mildred,
London, using their correct names.

Letters reveal that in 1792 Henry and Sarah were out and about in
society. Travelling to London, Bath and Burghley they must have shaken
off the monetary embarrassment. In fact, at about this time, fantastic
bills appeared: for clothes, jewels and livery for servants. Also, in 1792,
Sarah gave birth to a girl, called Sophia at 'the Peer's request'. She had a
round face and blue eyes and was 'just such a child as I could wish it'
according to her doting father.

The ninth Earl had expressed a wish that Sarah should 'bread' and she
fulfilled his wishes as best she could. As well as Sophia she produced two
other children in the years 1792–5. However, she suffered from some sort
of female complaint for which she was dosed with laudanum and brandy.
In poor physical health, and no doubt troubled by the lifestyle she was
forced to adopt, she gradually faded and to the desperate grief of her
husband died in January 1797.

In August 1800 Henry was married for the third time, to the Dowager
Duchess of Hamilton. She was, no doubt, a good stepmother for the three
little children and her portrait shows her to have a kindly face, but I
rather feel that with Sarah's death Henry was diminished. He certainly
adored her, and the great Lawrence portrait in the Billiard Room bears
testimony to that, showing them both in the best years of their married
life. Lord Tennyson's poem, *The Lord of Burleigh*, although a trifle trite,
tells the story of the courtship, marriage and Sarah's demise rather well.
I had it dinned into me as a child and would launch off at a moment's
notice, bringing tears of what I now know to be vexation to my listeners'
eyes.

Sarah did not live to see Henry elevated to the rank of Marquess,
which happened in 1801 in recognition of his charitable work.

## BROWNLOW, 2ND MARQUESS (1795–1867)

THE SECOND MARQUESS was not a very attractive character; in fact he could legitimately be described as a bit of a 'stinker'. His mother was the beautiful Sarah, the 'Cottage Countess', but he does not appear to have resembled his parents a great deal. He was only nine when he inherited and was under the guardianship of Lord St Helens, Evan Foulkes Esq., the Revd William Burslem and Lord Henniker. With the guidance of these worthy gentlemen he attained his majority. There was much rejoicing in Stamford including the pealing of bells and feasting in inns by the local populace. Had they all known what a second-rate individual he was, I daresay the celebrations might have been a little more muted.

*The 2nd Marquess*

The second Marquess was Groom of the Stole to Prince Albert for five years, resigning because of his opposition to the repeal of the Corn Laws in 1846 and the Act for the protection of native industry – both popular measures in the country. He had great political ambitions but his support of the interests of an aristocratic minority in the rotten borough of Stamford, combined with his habit of evicting tenants straight away if it was proved that they had voted for the opposition, did Burghley no good at all. He earned the cordial dislike of most people who knew him, which was not helped by his reputation as a man who ogled women in the town. In fact, his local standing was such that he had clods of earth thrown at his coach when he drove in the town and was forced to have two cannon mounted on the roof of the house, facing towards Stamford, in order to defend himself against the possibility of peasants in revolt.

The Marquess was well known for the racecourse which he reinstated between the Great North Road and Easton on the Hill, just outside Stamford. It had originally been created by the fifth Earl in the seventeenth century. Possessing some excellent horses, the Marquess entered for races and won the trophies which he had himself donated. He is the only member of the Jockey Club to be expelled and then reinstated, but we have never known what for.

The Marquess's wife, Isabella Poyntz, was a considerable heiress whose father lived at Cowdray Park in Sussex. She was very beautiful, according to her portrait by Sir Thomas Lawrence, but was reputed to be dull and 'very high' as Charles Dickens would have said. She was not popular. But she did provide the Marquess with eleven children, seven of whom survived.

## WILLIAM ALLEYNE, 3RD MARQUESS (1825–95)

THE THIRD MARQUESS is justly famous for his ability to squander money. He was a true hedonist with an enormous capacity for self-amusement. When he inherited the title in 1867 the Trustees had just sold a large amount of fenland to settle the debts created by the second Marquess. But by 1885 the third Marquess had debts of £330,000. The parties that were recorded at his London house were prodigious, and featured a barrel organ to which people danced 'incessantly'. A greater extravagance was his predilection for yachts – he owned two luxurious ones, the *Fawn* and the *Queen of Palmyra*. On the *Queen* he would go to the Mediterranean, calling in at resorts such as Biarritz on the way, and cruising around much as tycoons do today. On one voyage it is recorded that they got no further than the Isle of Wight, which they circumnavigated until the sherry ran out. Presumably this was a sea trial of some sort; maybe of His Lordship's liver.

The debts became so large that in 1888 the Dutch and Flemish pictures and the Chinese porcelain given to the family by Walter Ralegh were sold in a three-day sale at Christie's. The porcelain is now in the Metropolitan Museum of Art in New York. Alas, the sums achieved by the sale of all these precious things were trivial compared to what they would fetch today. However, the Italian seventeenth-century paintings attracted little interest so they all returned home, for which we are extremely grateful.

As well as the Christie's sale, land was disposed of and the yachts finally went too. But the Marquess had other interests. In one book of the period he is recorded as being 'An eminent pisciculturist ... and breeder of shorthorn cattle'. His pisciculture is evident by the installation of the trout hatchery at the top of the lake, which is now a famous obstacle in the cross-country phase of the Horse Trials. For this, no doubt, he should be congratulated.

*(left) The 3rd Marquess, (right) The 4th Marquess*

## BROWNLOW, 4TH MARQUESS (1849–98)

THE FOURTH MARQUESS only held the title for three years and is not particularly notable. In 1886, when still Lord Burghley, he presented his parents with a truly dreadful carved clock which was installed in the

Great Hall; it is still there. He was also responsible for having one of the treasures of Burghley incorrectly restored. He arranged for the pewter boulle table, made by Gerrit Jensen for the fifth Earl, to be cleaned and re-gilded. The capitals to the legs were then replaced, but upside down.

## BURGHLEY IN MY GRANDPARENTS' TIME

MY GRANDFATHER, the fifth Marquess of Exeter, inherited the title in 1898 and lived at Burghley until his death in 1956. He was a most dutiful and hardworking man who felt most keenly the great responsibility of the house and estate, and those who work here. I suspect that the worry of keeping the whole enterprise going, especially after World War II, must have been considerable. He was convinced that the future viability of an estate depended on how much land was owned. At a time when other landowners were selling up or allowing fields to lie fallow, he was exerting every effort to acquire more farms, taking them back in hand when tenants gave up and even purchasing odd bits here and there to increase his acreage.

The Marquess performed his job as head of a small empire to perfection. He was admired and regarded with a great deal of affection by those who worked on the estate. Almost every weekend his tenants would see him advancing into their farmyards, shoes polished to a glassy shine by Groves the butler, accompanied sometimes by Mutter, his agent. Mutter was shared between this estate and Aswarby, an estate which belonged to the Marquess's grandfather-in-law, near Bourne. Mutter, was, by all accounts, rather an odd character; short and rotund, he slept in the estate office here in Stamford during his Burghley 'days'. Once, when visited by his physician, he was found to be enthusiastically performing army-style exercises to improve his health, in the estate office, while wearing woollen combinations.

The Marquess shot pheasants, partridge and ground game when he had the chance but was more preoccupied with the effort he put into local affairs; he was indefatigable. Perhaps in an attempt to expunge the memory of the second Marquess, he spent hours on committees, chaired council meetings, and travelled all over the locality attending village functions. He was renowned for his wise counsel and approachability

*The 5th Marquess and Marchioness*

and rarely forgot a name or face.

My grandfather was not a snob and liked people, but he also liked everyone to fit comfortably into a set social slot, and would not, on any account, tolerate overfamiliarity. He had a very paternalistic attitude to those who worked for him, but if he ever caught someone out in a transgression which he considered to be underhand or deceitful he was unforgiving. For example, he had coal delivered to a yard in Stamford where bonafide Burghley employees could go and help themselves to however much they needed. Needless to say, it was discovered that this privilege was being abused by one or two employees who were supplying all and sundry. Eventually, although unwilling to believe that anyone would repay generosity in such a way, he was convinced it had happened and descended on the swindlers like an avenging angel: 'You deceived me, you stole from me, get out! OUT!' They never worked at Burghley again.

My grandfather's attitudes were, of course, the dying gasp of the Edwardian age, with its formality and pomposity. The social changes which occurred with such rapidity after World War I must have been difficult for him to adjust to. But in one respect at least, my grandparents were susceptible to modern fashion: health fads. For years my grandmother imbibed something called 'maté' which was a tea from Peru containing fairly large chunks of the coca plant, from whence cocaine. She found it most soothing, but wrote in her diary more than once 'Felt very slack today'; maybe as a result of the tea, who knows?

This was a time of cures for all sorts of illnesses which had not been thoroughly tested, and some of which were positively harmful, such as the deep x-rays used on my grandfather's painful arthritic hip. The treatment certainly eased the discomfort, but exposed his bladder to rays which could have been responsible for the cancer of the bladder which he eventually died from some time later.

My grandmother was born an Orde-Powlett (pronounced Orde-Porlet for unknown reasons). Her family home was Bolton Hall in Yorkshire. Looking through granny's daily diaries, it is obvious that she shared a working relationship with her husband. She was most conscious of her duties towards the employees and almost every entry has a mention of her visiting some elderly retired person or involvement in some charitable event or other. She was held in deep affection by those who worked for her which is well illustrated by a letter in 1928 thanking her for one she had sent to Mr E. Stacey: 'Thank you for all your kindness to me and

*My grandmother*

for the nice letter you sent me the morning of the operation, I shall always keep it, you was a friend and comforter. I prayed I should not get a cough as I don't know what would have happened if I had. I hope the dogs are well. Your obedient servant, E. Stacey.'

Family life at Burghley with four young children – David, Martin, Winifred and Romayne – can never have been dull. All the children lived up on the top west floor. There was a night nursery for the youngest and a day nursery in which Nanny and a succession of nursery maids held

*My grandparents at Bolton*

sway. There was a hip bath before the fire for washing in and a coal fire in all the rooms, serviced by a man whose arms were immensely long as a result, one presumes, of carrying heavy coal buckets up sixty-seven stairs several times a day.

Routine was everything; granny would visit the nursery in the morning and take the girls, once they were old enough, on the house rounds. This involved talking over menus with the cook, linen with the housekeeper, and steering clear of Groves, the fearsome butler. In 1901

*Children of the 5th Marquess: (l to r) Romayne, David, Winifred, Martin*

there were thirty indoor domestic staff, which by the early 1930s had shrunk to seventeen:

| | | |
|---|---|---|
| Housekeeper | Housemaids (5) | Kitchenmaids (2) |
| Head Housemaid | Dairymaid | Scullerymaid |
| Sewingmaid | Cook | Butler |
| Footman | Under Footman | Boy |

When the whole family was present at Burghley there was a Sunday routine which even now makes my Aunt Romayne shudder. After Church and lunch, grandpa and granny would don stout shoes and suitable clothes and set off on 'The Rounds'. Come rain or shine you *had* to attend. It began with the family pulling themselves across the lake on the ferry, then walking up the hill to the Dairy Farm and visiting the Woolhouses and the Robothams. Mr and Mrs Robotham had two daughters, Nellie and Eva, both very charming ladies with a terrific sense of humour. Neither was married; Nellie worked down at the house in the linen room and Eva was in charge of the dairy where cream, butter and superb cheese were made.

Having checked on the welfare of all at the Dairy Farm, the group would wend its way up the hill for another half mile or so to the Keeper's House, where game rearing was discussed. Then the big walk to the kitchen gardens and inspection of all the greenhouses, fruit trees, vegetable beds; and at last the start of the long walk home. The schools and almshouses in the town were supplied with free vegetables due to the excess production at this time.

Aunt Romayne reckons the round trip would have been about four miles. Hard work in tight buttoned boots when you are only seven. She has had rather an aversion to walking for fun ever since. As my cousin Michael Exeter remarked, it is terrible to think of all those people having to dress up and stay indoors and awake, thereby ruining any chance of a normal family Sunday, just because Lord and Lady Exeter chose to visit after lunch on that day. And every week!

Romayne hardly remembers David, my father, in the schoolroom because of the gap in their ages, but throughout his childhood he fought energetically with his elder sister Winifred. There are terrible tales of when, as a beastly small boy, he would whisper in her ear that he had a secret to tell her. He took her behind the heavy velvet curtains in the

*The Orangery in World War I*

sitting room and for a second, silence. Then a piercing shriek: 'He bited me, he bited me ...'

During World War I my grandfather was posted overseas to Egypt with his regiment. Burghley became a hospital for wounded soldiers. Reading my grandmother's diary for 1916, the year my grandfather went to Egypt, it seems that no one could have worked harder. Every minute of every day was absorbed with the management of the wards and entertaining those wounded soldiers who were well enough to go out. When we opened a large mahogany desk in the south passage after we moved in, it was filled to overflowing with notes of every meeting held by The Linen League, providers of bandages and hospital dressings in the 1914–18 war. My grandmother also had to cope with the numerous Church livings which fell vacant because the incumbents became service chaplains; she, as patron, had to find new vicars for those parishes.

The diary entry for 28 March 1916 notes: 'A tremendous blizzard the whole day till 6 p.m., a gale of hurricane force and blinding snow, drifts 6 ft deep in places, quantities of trees down, minus sixteen on one side alone of the low park avenue. More than 100 trees fell in less than five minutes in Burghley Park!' Also that year there is a passing mention of a zeppelin dropping a bomb between Blackstones and Newstead in Stamford, having circled over Burghley first. In April she went to call on her mother-in-law, 'who seemed very weak and insisted on giving me all her jewellery ...'

Entertainment at Burghley during the 1920s consisted of parties for shooting and hunting, or local charity balls. Large numbers of miles were covered by car in order to have lunch or tea or dinner with relations or friends. At Christmas and New Year much was made of joint parties for family and staff: dances, suppers and amateur dramatics were all popular and took place in the Great Hall. There was a certain rhythm to life to do with the seasons and farming. Hunting and shooting predominated in the winter and spring, and a great deal of riding was done by everyone. My grandmother was very elegant and looked superb when riding side-saddle. The girls and my father hunted almost continuously throughout the season, but Martin was not so keen. The weather is mentioned a great deal in my grandmother's diaries, as are the frequent 'hysteria attacks' suffered by one of the dogs, now thought to be due to faulty feeding.

You did not stay in the country, however, at the best time of year. In the early summer you went to London to 'do' the Season and see your friends. There was a London house at Rutland Terrace, and with the young ladies to be 'brought out', there was the usual round of tea parties, cocktails and balls. A great deal of time was also spent in the congenial pursuit of staying with relations who had house parties in the country. In the summer the whole family would go north for extended holidays to granny's family home, but I've also been told of a hot summer's day at Burghley when my grandmother swam on her back in the greenish waters of the lake, holding a parasol to ward off the rays of the sun.

*(opposite above) Members of the family at a meet in the early 1930s*

*(opposite below) My grandparents with Winifred and David before World War I*

*My grandparents' silver wedding anniversary in 1926*

In World War II the house was again used for the sick. The orangery was utilized as a convalescent ward, and recently a lady, whose grandfather had been looked after here, came and introduced herself to me. He had happy memories of warm summer days spent fisihng in the lake, when medical conditions allowed.

During the war the number of servants declined, but even so, in 1941 there were eleven, all women except for Groves the butler and the Boy. Groves was paid an annual salary of £120, a figure which never varied in the ten years recorded in the accounts ledger. The Boy's salary also remained static at £30 per annum. Eleven was really a skeleton staff considering that all meals would be served, my grandmother had a full-time lady's maid and my grandfather a valet. Standards however had to be kept up. A distant cousin of ours came as a child to dine at Burghley at the height of the war. He remembers a long difficult drive with no lights, a dark and very cold house with blackout curtains and rooms full of furniture covered in dust sheets. Dinner was served in the small and easily heated housekeeper's room by a butler and someone else (presumably the Boy). The food was disgusting and rather cold but it was eaten off silver-gilt eighteenth-century plates. He never forgot it.

At the beginning of the war the house was stripped in case of enemy action. Dr Till recalls the yard near the house filled with the enormous Georgian ale barrels from the cellar. They were removed in order that priceless paintings and other works of art could be stored below ground. Dozens of wooden packing cases were made by the estate carpenter, and everything from clocks to porcelain was wrapped and hidden. The fact that Hermann Goering had targeted Burghley as a prize for himself should Germany win the war no doubt added poignancy to the packing up of the treasures. Goering had also decided, my father found out after the war, that he was to be used as the sire of a race of athletic Aryans. Although amused, he was obviously absolutely appalled at the very concept. Given the fact that all his daughters have bandy legs and knock knees, and none can run, maybe he had good reason!

My grandparents took the modern view that if there was something you really wanted to do and were good at, then have a go. This was an enlightened outlook which incidentally did not pass into the next generation – I well recall the stony reception I had when I requested permission either to go on the stage via drama school or to study at the nearest art college. My father was supported in his athletic endeavours, while when Winifred turned out to have a marvellous singing voice, she was encouraged to go off to Italy to follow her career and had a wonderful time. She got a job singing at the Carla Rosa opera house in Milan. Uncle Martin told me a tale from sometime later when she lived in Albert Hall Mansions. She used to practise her scales in the bath. One morning there was a furious knocking on the front door of her flat. Rushing to answer it, wrapped in her bath towel, she was confronted by a furious neighbour – an Italian conductor whose face was daubed with bloodstained blobs of cotton wool. 'Please madame,' he begged, 'stop missing high C; every time you do that I cut myself shaving.'

My aunts have always been my favourite people. Both are exceptionally kind and have a particular sense of humour. When as a young girl I went to stay with Aunt Winifred Hotham, or Aunt Mutt as she was called by the family, at her lovely house near Beverley, it was very obvious that she ran the house virtually single handed, and it was very large. Trying to help by stacking and clearing the plates, I was appalled to hear an enraged auntly bellow from the scullery: 'What damn fool has stacked the plates? Now I shall have to wash the bottoms as well as the tops.'

It was in that house that we were armed with tennis rackets at the foot of the stairs to fight off the bats which colonized the nursery storey in the summer. Aunt Mutt is famous for the layered look in her clothes; I believe she once wore eleven articles of clothing on her upper half, for she hated the cold more than anything. Going to York races with her in later years had its moments too. She had terrible arthritis in her knees and took to crutches, on which she travelled at the speed of light. If an unwary fellow racegoer got in her way a crutch would be firmly applied to the small of his back and he would have to nip smartly out of the way or else.

Aunt Romayne Brassey has been a splendid successor to her father; she works tirelessly for the Red Cross and other charitable organizations in and around Stamford, and has been awarded the OBE in recognition of her many years' service for the Red Cross. She began her nursing career when she became a Red Cross nurse at the beginning of World War II.

Uncle Martin went out in 1930 to the British Columbian wilderness and created a profitable cattle ranch there on property bought by his father. The aura of success that surrounded my father when they were all growing up must have been difficult for Uncle Martin. However, when

*Michael, 8th Marquess (left) with his father, Martin (right), 7th Marquess*

my father's first marriage sadly ended in scandal, pain, recriminations and terrible disappointment among his nearest relations, it was Martin who was first prepared to accept my mother.

Following the death of his first wife, my cousin Michael's mother, in 1954, Martin and his second wife took into their home the three orphaned children of a remarkable man called Lloyd Meeker, who had been killed in a plane crash. Lloyd had a considerable following in America, helping and advising a growing community of people who had found something lacking in their lives. When Lloyd died, Uncle Martin took up the leadership, with many misgivings, but proved to have a great gift for spiritual counselling. There, in the stupendous scenery of the Rocky Mountains, he and his wife were able to share in a lifestyle which gave much and only required an open mind and willingness to work for the overall good. Although farming is the main enterprise, the group, who now have worldwide support under the name of The Emissaries of Divine Light, are engaged in hotel management, ski resort organization and other commercial activities.

During the war, because his parents were in Canada, my cousin Michael was billeted at Burghley during his school holidays. There must have been an enormous difference between life here and life in Canada. Here all was formality, unemotional behaviour, stiff collars and stiff servants. A really beastly room was provided for his use, and I can only guess at the dread he must have felt on coming to this house from Eton. Quite why granny treated him with such a lack of understanding, I cannot imagine, but the effect on his feelings for this house is obvious. Nonetheless, Michael and his family come and stay regularly now. I hope he finds it more congenial than he did then.

Michael inherited the title in 1988 when Uncle Martin died and handles his roles as head of the Emissaries (he is married to Lloyd Meeker's daughter Nancy) and Marquess of Exeter with great dignity. He has given his maiden speech in the House of Lords and is now an established member there. When he was Lord Burghley, before inheriting the marquessate, one of the tasks which gave him the most pleasure was opening the pub of that name in Stamford. His son Anthony, born in 1970, now in his turn Lord Burghley, read physiology at Oxford.

# CHAPTER FOUR

# THE STATE ROOMS

The rooms are described in the order encountered by a visitor on a conducted tour.

## THE OLD KITCHEN

THE OLD KITCHEN AT BURGHLEY is exactly what every visitor to an Elizabethan house expects to see. Huge and vaulted, its stone walls are much scarred and soot stained, while copper jelly moulds and cooking pans are there in abundance, and gigantic serving platters appear to be waiting to be loaded with capons or sides of beef. The number of copper jelly and pâté moulds should not surprise us, for in the eighteenth and early nineteenth centuries people had bad teeth and could not chew easily; hence the sloshed-up food, brawn and arrowroot moulds and so forth.

The kitchen also contains some oddities; none more so than the macabre collection of turtle skulls whose owners went into the soup tureen that is shaped, as if there were any doubt in the matter, like a turtle. I've always thought how lucky it was that the ancestors did not keep the bones of everything they ate – otherwise we could have been in trouble.

Hanging on the west wall is perhaps the only painting large enough to cope with the space, and with a suitable subject. Once considered to be by Rubens, it was revealed by recent restoration to bear the signature of Frans Snyders who shared his studio. The canvas shows a huge ox carcase, trimmed and ready for roasting in some vast oven. Rather out of scale, an embarrassed family of cats plays beneath the carcase, and behind them, through an open door, peers the inquisitive face of a dog, while in the garden a faint figure of a gardener clips the topiary.

On another wall there is a lugubrious elk head; at least I have always

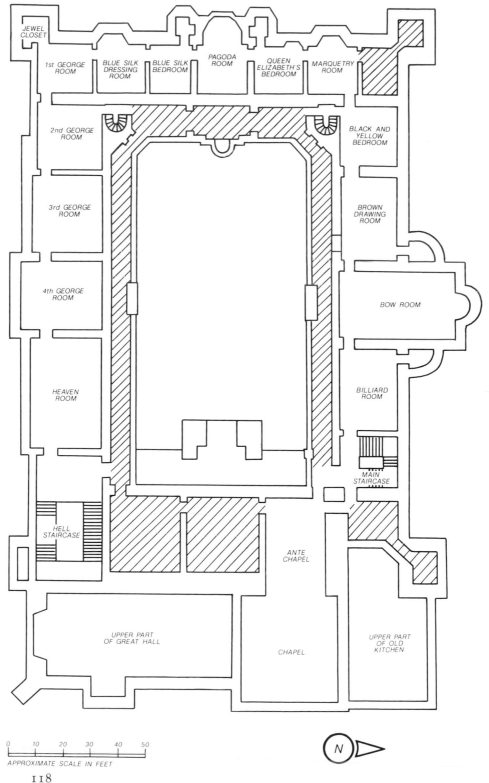

JEWEL
CLOSET

1st GEORGE
ROOM

BLUE SILK
DRESSING
ROOM

BLUE SILK
BEDROOM

PAGODA
ROOM

QUEEN
ELIZABETH'S
BEDROOM

MARQUETRY
ROOM

2nd GEORGE
ROOM

BLACK AND
YELLOW
BEDROOM

3rd GEORGE
ROOM

BROWN
DRAWING
ROOM

4th GEORGE
ROOM

BOW ROOM

HEAVEN
ROOM

BILLIARD
ROOM

MAIN
STAIRCASE

HELL
STAIRCASE

ANTE
CHAPEL

UPPER PART
OF GREAT HALL

CHAPEL

UPPER PART
OF OLD
KITCHEN

0    10    20    30    40    50

APPROXIMATE SCALE IN FEET

N

supposed it to be an elk and not a gnu. My mother, true to her name Diana, was a huntress and shot it in Sweden. She had a farm there, at Aleby, before the war, when she was still married to her first husband. I don't know how she came to have the farm, but maybe it was her friend Lilian Craig, who in turn was a friend at that time of Prince Bertil of Sweden (and later became his wife), who persuaded her into it.

The rather tetchy sign which reads, 'It is expressly ordered by his Lordship that no servants shall enter the kitchen except on business or remain longer than is necessary to perform what they have to do' hangs over one of the large black ranges, and serves to illustrate what life must have been like in those days when there was bustle and activity: scullions rushing here and there with vegetables from the garden, men bringing in the newly jointed lamb and beef, little maids with running noses and chilblains scouring copper pans with sand until they shone. Everywhere there would have been heat and noise and the wonderful smell of baking bread and fragrant stews, and in the middle of this a large fat cook, laying about him with a rolling pin when something went wrong, and trying to stop the constant stream of cold and hungry outdoor servants from chatting up the kitchen girls on the off chance of a peck on the cheek and a slice of fresh bread and cheese.

The octagonal opening, or lantern, in the ceiling, which casts light on the whole room, was hidden from sight until 1984. A friend from Sotheby's, Mark Armstrong, was living in one of the flats upstairs at the time. It had a curiously shaped bathroom with an octagonal compartment. We had idly discussed installing a shower in it. One day, full of the joys of spring, Mark jumped out of the bath and chanced to look down. To his horror, there was a creak and a groan and he could see the public standing about sixty feet below him in the Old Kitchen. Keeping calm, he tiptoed across the room and rang to tell us. The floor was quite rotten, full of worm, and could have let him fall through in a rather biblical fashion at any time. The octagonal area in the bathroom was in fact the lantern which had been boarded up in the nineteenth century and lost to memory.

*(opposite) Floor plan of the State Rooms today*

## HOGS HALL

GOING FROM THE OLD KITCHEN to the first floor you have to go through the Hogs Hall, so-called because, presumably, the flitches of bacon hung there. Bells all over the walls give an idea of the housekeeper's life and that of the housemaids in times past. 'Jangle, jangle', 'Now what does that old fool up in the Brown Drawing Room want?' You can imagine the scene. Also in here is the Telephone Office. Smaller than a public telephone kiosk, in the 1950s it was the only place in the house where there was an 'instrument' and the perishingly cold conditions of its location served to keep the bills as low as the temperature.

You then go up the stone stairs; called the Roman Staircase, after the original architectural description of *scala Romana*, the name can cause confusion. We were once having lunch in the dining room next door and overheard the statement: 'Ladies and Gentlemen, please come this way. This is our Roman staircase, it's Tudor ...' There was a justifiable silence from the group. I hope they sorted it out later. There is a rather jolly print from Joseph Nash's *Mansions of England* showing the first Lord Burghley on this staircase, well wrapped up against the cold, perhaps coming down from having inspected his wonderful roof; I like to imagine him there.

## THE CHAPEL AND ANTE-CHAPEL

THE MOMENT YOU ENTER the Ante-Chapel, the next room on the tour, you cannot help but wonder what happened to the sixteenth and seventeenth centuries. The whole size, shape and decorative detail is that of about 1760. One of the causes of the transformation from what was here before was Horace Walpole, who visited the house in the early eighteenth century and commented that Burghley was pretty fine overall but that the 'Chapel is a low, dark and ill-favoured room', a comment which obviously stung the family and encouraged them to update these rooms. The Ante-Chapel is separated from the main Chapel by an arched, pierced wall which allowed those lowly persons who came to services to observe without impinging upon the family. I am sure that in Victorian days every member of the household, and outside workers where practicable, would have been expected to attend daily prayers.

Even when my father and his brother and sisters were young attendance was obligatory. My Aunt Winifred swore she could wash, put her hair up and be in the Chapel in eight minutes flat from her room at the other end of the house. I love to imagine the pounding feet and the breathless arrival of the children just in time not to be shut out by the elderly butler. Prayers were announced by the ringing of the gong which hangs in the inner courtyard on a stout wooden frame, carved with the word 'Gong' in case anyone was in doubt.

When I was young the routine had relaxed a little. We still had prayers at 9.15 a.m. but only three times a week. Attendance was still obligatory. If you missed prayers, you missed breakfast: a great spur to religion. The men always sat on the right of the aisle and the women on the left, to keep their minds on higher things and to discourage familiar-ity. We used the 1662 spoken morning prayer service, suitably sur-rounded by the soaring extravagance of Catholic baroque art, with naked ladies everywhere, plucking a fair-haired Moses from the bullrushes and dancing before Solomon, giving the firm impression that idolatry was rather jolly. These, together with a painting by Carl Loth of a revoltingly wrinkled Witch of Endor, all served nicely to distract one's attention from what was going on.

We like to continue the use of this family chapel whenever we can. The days of thrice weekly prayers have gone; we do not have the vicar of St Martin's, ex-officio Chaplain to the house, arriving in his surplice on a Triumph motor bike like Elijah, as the Revd Parker used to do. We do however have satisfactory christenings, Good Friday prayers, and some-times funerals there. We have always felt that it is just and proper, if the relatives desire it, that anyone working on the estate should be able to have their funeral in the Chapel.

The enormous altarpiece by Paolo Veronese, depicting Zebedee's wife petitioning Our Lord, was bought specifically for the Chapel by the ninth Earl, and it came to Burghley with a fine pair of matching organ doors from a small church on the Venetian island of Murano. As so often in this house, there is the fascinating question of how a painting of this size was moved, because it is about twelve feet high by six feet – not a trifle.

The Chapel seat furniture used to appear under the ubiquitous heading of 'Chippendale' in the guidebook. In fact it is to a design by Chippendale but made by Messrs Ince and Mayhew, who supplied the ninth Earl with many pieces of furniture, all of superb quality. We would never have known this but for foraging in a chest of drawers and finding a petulant letter from the ninth Earl to his sister, Lady Betty Chaplin, asking her to instruct Mr Mayhew to hurry up with the seats of the Chapel because he had already waited too long.

Hanging in the Ante-Chapel is an enormous painting by the seventeenth-century Italian artist Mattia Preti. He had a prolific career and worked in many parts of Italy before moving to Malta in 1661. He was responsible for the series of frescoes in the Cathedral of St John in Valletta and was made a Knight of Malta. This painting, dating from about 1680, depicts the Triumph of Time and is highly symbolic. In 1958 it was valued for probate at £28. The 1992 valuation was in the region of £250,000. It was this painting which our friends from Seibu, the department store in Tokyo, paid to be restored as part of their sponsorship.

Music in the Chapel was impossible when I was young. The harmonium suffered from incurable bronchitis and still does, the cure being too expensive to consider. The organola, invented before electricity, takes two strong men to get it turning. The beautiful chamber organ, housed in a harpsichord case, was made for the ninth Earl by William Grey in 1790. The ninth Earl was very keen on music (he was a good friend of Handel and contributed to the composer's memorial in Westminster Abbey) and when the muse came upon him, which it sometimes did in the stilly night after the odd glass of port, he would ring for his wretched butler who would stumble downstairs half asleep and pump the bellows of the organ for his Lordship while the latter waded through Handel and Vivaldi with enthusiasm. There is no record of his being any good at playing but then the butler would hardly give an unbiased account, having been dragged from a warm bed to perform this thankless task.

The organ was found to have a dead sparrow in the bellows when the Sotheby's expert tried to rouse it to life while listing the house contents in 1983. Since then, however, with the enthusiastic help and advice of Gerald Gifford, Master of Music at Wolfson College, Cambridge, we have had it repaired. Gerald comes and gives recitals on it from time to time and also plays it for our Christmas carol concert, a very popular event involving Miranda and my half-brother Anthony Forbes singing solos and about 150 people all singing carols fit to bust.

## THE BILLIARD ROOM

THIS ELEGANT ROOM IS another example of the ninth Earl's taste. He employed Lancelot 'Capability' Brown not only as a landscape gardener but also as a mentor on interior design. In the 1760s Brown was responsible for drawing the Earl's attention to the volume published by Robert Wood in 1753 containing the illustrations of the ruins at Palmyra. It is possible that the classical ceiling in this room was derived from this source. It is worth noting that the designs taken from these ruins also had an enormous effect on late-eighteenth-century furniture design, not only in England; 'Palmyra' scrolls were recorded in 1769 in the Philadelphia furniture collection of John Cadwalader, a great collector.

I remember going through here as a child with my father and listening to an opinionated Yorkshireman, obviously an 'expert' on portraits: 'Now pay attention Mother, see all these ladies in low dresses? Well, they weren't any better than they should be: they were all Charles II's mistresses.' 'Oh, I do hope not,' murmured my father, 'they are all relations of mine.'

The three most important men in the history of the house, after William Cecil, the Builder, have their portraits in this room. They are John, the fifth Earl of Exeter, and the ninth and tenth Earls. Hanging above the fireplace is the marvellous picture by Sir Thomas Lawrence of the tenth Earl and his wife – the so-called 'Cottage Countess'.

Beneath the portraits of the fifth Earl and his Countess hangs the whiskery and benevolent countenance of Doctor Willis. He was an eighteenth-century local physician who ministered to poor tormented George III during his bouts of insanity caused by hereditary porphyria. The treatment for almost every complaint in those days seems to have involved 'the physic, the black draught and leeches'. In all these remedies Dr Willis no doubt excelled. He managed to retain his popularity with the Cecil family, in spite of these nostrums, for they purchased a mourning ring in his memory when he died; it is still here.

His pastel portrait and its companion of Miss Hauchcorne, governess to the children of the 'Cottage Countess', are superb examples of this particular art form, often overlooked by collectors today. The artist, John Russell, was not only skilled with pastels, he also was by way of being an inventor and managed to stitch up Henry, the tenth Earl, persuading him to buy his patent 'Selenograph' (an instrument for examining and obtaining pictures of the moon's surface). We found it, obviously regretted by the buyer, lying in the 'Dark Nurseries', beneath heaps of assorted clutter, in 1985, still wrapped in eighteenth-century paper and hairy string with the packing case marked with instructions to 'Change horses at Bedford'.

John Russell's account of his reception by the Earl and the difficulties he had finding his way about Burghley are amusing. His diary records: 'In the morning paid my respects at Burleigh, the polite Earl received me more like a friend than an employer. I was struck with the spacious domain; its lofty spire, tower-like turret, numerous pinnacles and ornamental chimneys, gave, with its uncommon magnitude, more the appearance of a town than a house.' Once inside, he continues: 'The convenience of the inside answers to the exhibition without this noble mansion ... I have several times been lost going about the house, so as to be obliged to call to servants passing to tell me the way to my apartments. His Lordship's sideboard of plate is very grand, of gold and silver; the silver cistern, the largest I ever saw, has a carpet on the inside, to prevent noise I suppose from the bottles. My bedroom I have not yet entered as I mean not to sleep there before Monday. I dread being lost in the way by night when I do go, as it is assigned at a great distance from the room in which I am employed. My greatcoat and umbrella were taken there when I first entered the house, and a servant was sent for them when I was about to return to Stamford; he said it was half a mile off ... I waited until I was tired.'

A series of oval portraits hangs on the lower register, some with curious animals included. These are the bibulous members of a drinking and gambling club, patronized by the gentry and their acquaintances in the late seventeenth century. It was called the 'Little Bedlam' club, probably for obvious reasons. The members thought, perhaps foolishly, that if they called one another by the name of an animal the stories of their debauches would not be spread abroad by the servants. The fiery-tempered artist, Antonio Verrio, who painted many of the ceilings and walls at Burghley, and who was a member of the club, portrayed himself with his rather appropriate symbol: a porcupine.

## THE BOW ROOM

FOR YEARS THIS ROOM was erroneously known as 'The Ball Room'. This was patently ridiculous, firstly because of the relatively small size of the room and secondly because, had anyone tried to have a decent party in here, they would have gone straight through the floor because until 1990 the joists were not in contact with the walls.

This room was painted by Louis Laguerre, Louis XIV's godson. Employed at Burghley from 1697 in company with his son-in-law, Jean Tijou, Laguerre decorated this room in truly splendid and martial style. At one time the room was intended for use as the State Dining Room, and is so described in the 1688 inventory. By the eighteenth century, it was in use as a music room and soirées were held here by the ninth Earl. One can only hope he was not actually performing, for even if his nocturnal practising with the butler had been successful he would hardly have been of concert standard.

During the nineteenth century the Victorians found a much more sober use for the room. It was here that the Congress of Berlin was drawn up by Disraeli (a friend of the family), when Prime Minister, in 1878. A reflective portrait of the great man is in here and even a white glass goblet which commemorates the event. It is of such blinding mediocrity that I could not resist purchasing it.

Not at all overshadowed by past happenings, my father and his brother used to play billiards here while their elders were playing more calmly next door. Wild games of 'Billiard Fives' were reported. Chips of seventeenth-century paint fell to the ground like confetti as ivory balls whizzed about wreaking appalling damage. Shoe polish was employed to disguise the holes and it is only now, after 3000 man hours of restoration under the able direction of Michael Cowell our picture conservator, that we can begin to appreciate the quality of Laguerre's design.

## THE BROWN DRAWING ROOM

FOR REASONS NEVER SATISFACTORILY explained to us, this room, in spite of its title, was always pink. The guides were driven nearly insane with repeated questions as to why, and so, to everyone's enormous relief, when the budget allowed, we redecorated it ... brown.

There are thirty-one pre-1700 plaster-moulded ceilings similar to this one at Burghley, all recorded as the work of Edward Marten. Bits drop off quite frequently which explains the eager entreaties of the guides to look up. This is not merely to admire the intricate convolutions of twining vines and roses, but to make sure that you are not going to be obliterated by a pomegranate.

One of the biggest problems we have, incidentally, is with elderly persons who gaze upwards for too long, thus constricting the arteries in their necks which causes them to pass out and fall over. This not only poses a risk to other visitors but can damage the furniture ...

It may seem a bit strange that there is a bed in the Brown Drawing Room, since the house is not so bereft of sleeping accommodation that we have to bed guests down in living rooms. But it was here that Princess Victoria slept when she visited the house in 1835 when a girl. Her mother had a fixation that they should, whenever possible, share a bedroom. At Burghley this was ruled out because the bedroom next door was too small. So a compromise was reached and the princess slept in the brass bed, specially hung with crimson silk, in this drawing room. I believe one of the first things that Victoria did on becoming Queen was to alter this sleeping arrangement, much to her mother's unease.

The beautiful, cut-glass chandelier in here has a slightly odd history. When Simon and I moved in, it hung downstairs in the family sitting room where it seemed rather grand and out of place. We walked round the house and, after much discussion, hung it where it is now. Two years later I found a faded photograph taken about 1900 showing the chandelier exactly here.

It is interesting to note that a similar thing happened with two portraits, only this time the other way round. We loved the portraits of Angelica Kauffman by Nathaniel Dance and David Garrick by Kauffman so much that we pinched them from the public rooms and hung them in the family sitting room, on the new turquoise fabric covering the previously yellow wall. An engraving of the room, done in the early nineteenth century, shows the two pictures on the same wall, in the same position. We also found that, prior to being yellow, the walls had always been turquoise.

The Brown Drawing Room contains quite a few English pictures. A pair of portraits by Thomas Gainsborough show Sir Christopher Which-cote Bt and his wife, ancestors of the fourth Marchioness. She has rather a delicate, if insipid face, but the white dog with his paw on her knee is a triumph. The story is that when Gainsborough was fed up with the sitter he would concentrate on the dog. In this instance I fear her conversation had palled on the artist for the painting is a canine masterpiece.

During World War II a bomb fell in the park about 200 yards from the house, blowing in all the windows in several rooms on this north front. It is fortunate, therefore, that the painting on glass, by Margaret Pierson of Newcastle, survived the action and can still be appreciated in its position fastened between two window mullions. It is by way of being a 'Curiosity', signed and dated 1789. She copied it after Wright of Derby.

Eighteenth-century English serpentine commodes have become much sought after and in here we have two excellent examples. However, the irritation is that we have no real idea who made them. The firm of Ince and Mayhew were much employed by the ninth Earl. So was a man called Wortley Searson who sold everything from furniture to cheese. The company of Newton and Fell are also in evidence in the accounts, providing panelling, picture frames, beds and so on. The amount of money paid out to suppliers of fine English furniture in the years 1760–93 was enormous and, unfortunately, these commodes could have been made by anyone. There are six in the house altogether, dotted round the State Rooms, all with slightly varying ormolu mounts. It will be a good day when we run a receipt to ground.

The same 'who made it?' question applies to the extraordinary pier glass and console table. With not a straight line in either, they stand testimony to the mad frenzy of a demented carver using every acanthus, garland, ho-ho bird, flower and even monkey that his imagination could conceive, and all gilt and as fragile as a butterfly. When we hung the wallpaper in here we stuffed it behind the carving with a knife blade, for we were not going to take the mirror off the wall and risk losing the whole lot.

## THE BLACK AND YELLOW BEDROOM

THIS ROOM IS DOMINATED BY the stupendous four-poster bed, one of five remaining in the house. From the earliest days of domestic furnishing, the bed has been extremely important in the English house; probably the most expensive object you would own, and one with much social 'cachet' attached. There were special beds for being born in, dying in, consummating marriage in and pure showing off in. The latter category was definitely that to which this bed belonged.

Since the creation of these suites of state apartments in the seventeenth century, beds like this one have had pride of place for the use of honoured guests. Like many other similar beds it has been refurbished two or three times in its lifetime. You can imagine the conversation at breakfast: 'Oh, my word. The Princess Royal is coming to stay ... Let's get the bed done up.' Off it would go to London to have the tired old silks cleaned and re-attached, the headboard re-embroidered and the 'Counterpoint' (bedspread) re-quilted. Then the date of the royal visit might be embroidered very large on the canopy. Let us hope no one cancelled a visit at short notice. In fact this may have happened in this instance, because the date embroidered is 1838 but Queen Adelaide only got here in 1842.

The triumphant plumes atop the tester in this splendid creation are amazing. Made from thin ribbons of solid silver, bent and bound into fantastical floral shapes, and here and there enlivened with the remaining scarlet silk, they really show that this was a No. 1 bed. The hangings once all matched, with a background of black silk satin beneath the applied sprays of dazzling silken, padded flowers. The linings of the curtains were a brilliant primrose yellow. Mattress upon mattress made certain that those with weak backs were unable to walk at all the morning after the night spent shrouded inside these elegant curtains, but my goodness the bed was grand.

HM King George VI and HM Queen Elizabeth were the last royal visitors to sample the bed, when, as Duke and Duchess of York, they stayed at Burghley. In 1986 we had the pleasure of a visit from HM Queen Elizabeth the Queen Mother. The idea was to revisit the room which she had occupied so long ago with the King. It was a freezing day; snow was thick on the ground and drifts almost prevented the car from leaving Sandringham. The State Rooms at Burghley are not heated – it would make no economic sense to make them so because they are closed to the public in the winter – with the result that the temperature on this day was arctic.

The Queen Mother arrived looking smashing, accompanied by my half-sister Angela Oswald, her lady-in-waiting, and my brother-in-law, Michael Oswald, her racing manager. Her Majesty was wearing a dress, a

*The Old Kitchen, one of the oldest parts of the house*

*View of the south front in winter*

cardigan and, of course, a hat. We were appalled. 'Ma'am,' we murmured, 'it's freezing upstairs, wouldn't you like to borrow a coat?', 'A coat? My word, no thank you, I've got my woolly on', she replied. We set off upstairs. The temperature was, in fact, well below freezing; our breath hung in clouds and our fingers went first blue then white. It was hard to talk without your teeth chattering, while ahead the gracious figure walked, oblivious of the climate, exclaiming over everything, missing nothing. Finally we arrived in the Black and Yellow Bedroom. There was a pause. 'Is this it? Really? Do you know I don't recall it; of course it was dark when we were here.'

We carried on round the house and, nearly at the end both of our cold weather endurance and the tour, she turned to us and with a delightful smile remarked: 'Do you know, this house is very *bracing.*' We concurred, quickened our pace to the lower floor and blessed warmth and a thawing drink. Later we received a charming note to tell us she had remembered the room vividly on the way back to Sandringham.

The Soho 'grotesque' tapestries were woven by special order of the fifth Earl of Exeter when he was remaking the interiors on this floor of the house in the seventeenth century. His dream was to create a new house from the long galleries and draughty, inconvenient chambers left over from the Elizabethan age. In Italy and France he had seen the way that rooms were furnished and hung with textiles and had even ordered some tapestries from the Gobelins factory in Paris. However, John Vanderbank, the chief weaver for Charles II in London, is rumoured to have had a workshop in Stamford, although little is known about it. In any event, Vanderbank was commissioned by the Earl to furnish his new rooms with the best tapestries and they are one of Burghley's greatest glories.

To restore these great hangings we employed a tapestry restorer, Michael McGreal, who lived and worked in a cottage in the park. He came to us from Dalmeny in Scotland, where he had been working. His stitching and colour matching were the best, and he even dyed his own yarns with natural vegetable dyes to match the originals. The great secret is to keep re-weaving to a minimum, because the new colours do not always fade to the same shades as the originals and can look awful after the passage of time.

The tapestry behind the bed in this room has retained its colour well because of lack of exposure to light. When our sponsors from Seibu, Tokyo, were looking for a dramatic wall covering for our mini 'Treasure Houses' exhibition, they fell in love with this tapestry. Feeling like murderers, we allowed the careful packers to put it in a box and for the first time in its life (and I rather hope the last), this treasure, made in 1680 or thereabouts, whizzed off to Japan to go on exhibition. It must be my Scottish blood but I hate lending things from the house, although our borrowers have been generosity itself, and somehow we have to raise the badly needed funds for restoration.

The great plumbing revolution of the nineteenth century affected this room as much as any other in the house. The second Marquess (1795–1867), dubious though he was in other matters, cunningly inserted a wash-down closet in the thickness of the panelling. He also, less praiseworthily, sliced a hole in the Soho tapestry near the door into the next room, in order to allow access to his new bathroom in the service passage which runs round on the inside of all these rooms. No doubt this manoeuvre was heartily applauded by his house-guests but to us, conservationists all, it was a heretical thing to do.

The Triumph of Time *by Mattia Preti*

*(opposite) The Ante-Chapel. The plasterwork ceilings here and in the Chapel were designed by Lancelot 'Capability' Brown*

The large Japanese Imari jars standing on either side of the fireplace bear witness to the collecting mania for things oriental in the seventeenth century. The fifth Earl's taste was pretty well faultless. Although these large pieces were in all probability bought to impress the neighbours as much as for their intrinsic beauty, they were, of their type, the top of the range and would have been extremely expensive.

The thirst for oriental porcelain had been slaked for many years by the importation of Chinese works of art. Supplies came from the East India Company, among others, until the civil war in China, in about 1640, caused problems with delivery and production. There had been no real competition from Japan. Gradually, during the 1650s, the trading carried out by the Dutch in Japan began to bear fruit. By the beginning of the 1660s enamel ware from Arita was being seen in Europe for the first time.

We know so little of the methods of purchase used by the gentry in those days. Did they make use of a 'China Man', who was an agent with a shop or go-down near the docks, or did they receive visits from a porcelain trader in a coach who trundled up and down the main roads of England, much as certain Eastern gentlemen in Mercedes sell Indian carpets nowadays? Whatever method was employed, the curious thing is that the same objects, give or take, turn up in large houses to the right and left of main roads from London to Edinburgh and beyond.

The brocade Imari patterns on the jars are stylized and were reproduced over and over again by every manufacturer from Samson to Wedgwood, but the figures of animals and humans made by the Japanese in the heyday of their production in the seventeenth century could not be bettered by anyone. In the next room is a representative selection of some of the best.


## THE MARQUETRY ROOM

THE STEPPED corner chimneypiece first appeared in the seventeenth-century designs of Daniel Marot. It was adopted by many owners of great houses as an ingenious way of using space to set off their newly acquired and very expensive collections of oriental porcelain. The organizers of the 'Treasure Houses of Britain' exhibition in Washington, DC, in 1985, copied the shelving design from a Marot original. We were so impressed by the appearance of the Burghley pots when they were displayed there that we modelled this example on the American version.

On the top shelf are the Burghley wrestling boys. Only a few examples of this particular model are known. They do not represent, as one might surmise, sumo wrestlers, but young men called into the potter's workshop to act as models. A Japanese man once told me that their underpants were not the correct type for sumo. You learn something new every day.

When the fifth Earl bought the Japanese porcelain, he was not only following the current fashion but also indulging his or his wife's taste for amusing figures. The puppies and the elephants are a case in point. Vigorous and lifelike except for the palette of iron red, turquoise and blue with which they are coloured, they obviously gave the potter much pleasure to make and equally great pleasure to successive Lady Exeters, who have had them on the mantelpiece in their dressing room since the seventeenth century. They were still there when my mother moved in in 1956.

The interior design of this room was inspired by the discovery of the 1738 inventory, which stated that: 'The rooms along the west front of the house are painted to resemble the marble of the chimneys' – probably a decorative scheme introduced by the fifth Earl. We felt that the re-marbling of the panelled areas of the walls was, therefore, an historical necessity. The only problem was that the chimney in this room is a particularly dreary shade of mottled greyish black. It was not a cheery prospect.

The correct decision in the circumstances seemed to be a little artistic licence. We took the dark moss green from the Flemish paintings and, using a chrysanthemum leaf from a handy pot plant on the chest of drawers, were able to ask the Gainsborough Silk Weaving Company to dye fabric to match to go on the walls. We then asked Eddie Goodridge, a local specialist in decorative paint finishes, to marble the woodwork in shades of toning green. Although there is an unhealthy tendency nowadays slavishly to copy the colour and patterns of the past when it comes to redecoration, I felt that in this instance the seventeenth-century conceit was worth repeating, and it seems to form a good backdrop for the furniture and paintings.

*(overleaf) The Chapel, with altarpiece by Paolo Veronese.*

From the title of the room it is evident that marquetry furniture is close at hand. The technique of laying different coloured veneers one onto another and then cutting through the multi-hued sandwich to create the backgrounds and shapes in order to decorate cupboards, chests, tables and chairs, was at its peak in the seventeenth century. Sometimes described as Anglo-Dutch, to cover Dutchmen working in England and vice versa, it is a staggeringly attractive skill, especially when seen on a large surface such as the table in the window. It is hard to believe the fineness of the steel blades that are required to cut the tendrils and petals which make up the pattern. If the sun had never shone on the finished article, we might have been able to enjoy a variety of colours rather than just the shades of brown. But we do know where the chairs were made; when one of the leaves fell off the splat, a piece of Dutch newspaper was revealed underneath.

Graham Child, a director of Sotheby's Furniture Department, discovered that the oval marquetry table described above was made from a floor panel. It was a glamorous seventeenth-century practice to inlay the floor as well as the furniture. We know from an entry in the 1688 inventory that the room known as 'My Lady's Closett' was decorated in this way. The table top is 'cradled' on the reverse, a method of construction which seems to corroborate the provenance.

Wood is a very tactile substance. It is most satisfactory to stroke a piece of walnut which has been lovingly polished by successive housemaids since its purchase in 1690. One piece that would not appreciate being loved in this way, however, is enclosed in a glass case and hangs near the door into Queen Elizabeth's Bedroom. It is a model of a small dead bird, suspended on a thread from a nail, with a bluebottle on its neck, and is about five inches high. It was carved from a single piece of wood at the end of the eighteenth century by a Frenchman called Jean Demontreuil who worked in the Faubourg St Honoré and exhibited at the Paris Salon. He occasionally used marble and terracotta as well as wood. Rumour has it that he went blind in middle age and, looking at this example of his work, it is easy to see why.

Beside this intricate carving is another of Burghley's great treasures: a painting by Pieter Brueghel the Younger, called *Rent Day*. In almost miniaturist style, the artist shows us a room filled with peasants coming to pay their dues to their landlord's agent. The room is lit by a small window partially glazed with opaque green glass, the other panes obscured by oiled paper. The walls are hung with hempen ropes to absorb the moisture generated by so many unwashed bodies, which otherwise would cause the rent rolls and other documents to become soggy. The agent, wearing a velvet cap, sits arrogantly behind the desk listening with a bored demeanour to the tale of hardship being poured into his ear by one of the cringing peasants. Outside the half-open door, another peasant peers through the crack to judge what mood the agent may be in today. In the foreground a woman brings out of a sack her offering of berries, while her husband holds up a scrawny fowl. It is a powerful picture and was brought back to Burghley by Lord Newlands, who acquired it at a sale in Scotland and, recognizing it as one of the Flemish paintings sold in the nineteenth century from Burghley, generously gave it back.

The Dutch and Flemish paintings are the residue left in the house after the great sale of 1888. To read the catalogue of what was sold in order to meet the family debts is a sobering experience. The list of Van Dycks, Brueghels, Rubenses, Titians, Raphaels and da Vincis makes the mouth water. The only consolation is that at this period people were not accurate with attributions and names may have been a bit optimistic.

And it would appear that even if they could not sell their possessions, the relations were quite happy to give them away in a good cause. For example, I found a letter addressed to my grandfather: 'My Dear Marquess, You may be aware that I was the fortunate winner of the lottery at the Red Cross Sale, to which your Lordship generously donated a painting by the artist Rubens. I would be most grateful if your Lordship could tell me a little about this work, where it was acquired etc.' The terrifying part is that my grandfather probably believed the painting was genuine.

## QUEEN ELIZABETH'S BEDROOM

EVERY SELF-RESPECTING Elizabethan house should boast a room slept in by the Virgin Queen. As is well known, she spent a great deal of time trailing round the countryside visiting, and bankrupting, her loyal subjects. The announcement that she was planning a stopover at Burghley in 1566 must have thrown her 'Secretary Cecil' into something of a panic. It was also his mother's residence and we cannot know how the old lady would have reacted to the impending invasion. Also the invasion planned was on an enormous scale.

The Billiard Room

(opposite) The Bow Room, originally planned as the State Dining Room
and decorated by Louis Laguerre

In a book we have here, which lists the Princess Elizabeth's possessions when she was shut in the Tower of London by her half-sister Mary, it is recorded that in her train, as well as innumerable courtiers and hangers on, there were two camels. You can imagine the conversation between two labourers lifting roots in a field as the cavalcade passed: 'I tell you what Horace, I don't think much of them horses what they have down in London.' Meantime the two humps undulating past above the stone wall with the superior dinosaur-like head on the end of the sinuous neck, must have been enough to convince any local to lay off the mead for a week or two.

One of the best chambers was prepared for the Queen, and extra victuals laid by for feeding the multitude, and no doubt Lady Cecil and her mother-in-law had new gowns made. Everyone waited for the honoured guest to arrive. Something then happened to wreck all the carefully laid plans; Ann, Sir William's daughter, developed smallpox. Disaster. There was no chance that the Queen would stay in the same house as such a deadly contagion. No doubt with much gnashing of teeth on the part of the host and hostess, it was decided to lodge the monarch at a nunnery in the town. Lady Cecil's efforts to spruce up the house, including preparing a beautiful room with rich hangings, and the organization of banquets and entertainments, were all in vain. It was fortunate, perhaps, that William was not basing the furtherance of his career on having Queen Elizabeth to stay; they knew each other too well for that and no doubt she appreciated his concern for her health, even if her fare was a little diminished as a result.

This cannot have been the original room prepared for the royal visit, as this part of the house was not built until some ten years later. For many years the superb full tester bed was called 'Queen Elizabeth's bed', but Sheila Landi, of the Victoria and Albert Museum, believes that it was constructed rather too late to have been used by the Queen and is probably nearer to mid seventeenth century. What is not disputed is the quality of the bed and the suite of chairs, both of which were restored for us from a totally wrecked state thanks to the generosity of Remy Martin.

The tapestries in here were ordered from the Gobelins factory by the fifth Earl of Exeter on his European travels. He had a rather strained relationship with Monsieur Jans at the Gobelins Paris workshops. Desperate letters between them exist, containing repeated requests for the money owing on the order. The hangings, of course, were not much good to anyone else because they were emblazoned with the Cecil family coat of arms, a fact of which the Earl was no doubt well aware.

There is a charming and probably apocryphal tale of a guide in a country house (not Burghley) who, when taking round a group of visitors and showing with great pride the splendid tapestries covering the walls, announced: 'Ladies and Gentlemen, please look at these wonderful and rare hangings, they were made by GOBLINS.'

On either side of the fireplace are two curious little wax bas-reliefs. Framed and glazed, they hung for years over the only radiator in the State Rooms. They have just survived, however, and bear the closest scrutiny which reveals tiny figures. One depicts the sacking of Rome and the other the rape of the Sabine women, which were favourite subjects for sculptors and artists.

My father used to relate a story of two old ladies sitting in a picture gallery, gazing at a painting showing desperate virgins being flung over horses by muscular raiders and men carrying off screaming maidens right, left and centre amid general mayhem. After a pause one old girl turned to the other and in a whisper said: 'You know, Maud, I think it must have been their jewels they were after.' I suppose in a manner of speaking she was quite correct.

At first glance the dressing table seems rather over decorated. It is painted in a pseudo-oriental style with a myriad coloured sprigs of flowers. Curious figures and buildings abound and the whole effect is most bizarre. The table is in fact a casualty of fashion from the seventeenth century. Once quite normal, it was decorated, probably by a member of the family, in the manner set out in the treatise published by Messrs Stalker and Parker in 1688. They advocated methods by which young ladies with time on their hands could 'improve' items of furniture.

The mirror which stands on this curious creature is a good example of stumpwork. The glass sadly has been replaced but the frame of laburnum encloses a border, rich in embroidery, dating from the seventeenth century and depicting all the usual dotty palaces, stiff royal figures and imaginative landscapes that delight those who appreciate this type of work.

In the tapestry at the back of the room, the scissors of the nineteenth-century vandals had been, until recent restorations, visibly at work. Behind this room, and all the others on this floor, runs the 'screens

*The Brown Drawing Room, with the bed slept in by Princess Victoria on a visit to Burghley in 1835*

passage' into which the second Marquess, followed by my grandmother, inserted 'spare' bathrooms and loos. My grandmother was once informed by the lugubrious house plumber that there was not enough room to put in a full-length bath. Narrowing her eyes, she thought over what he had said and then to his surprise she lay down on the floor. 'Draw round me' she instructed. He did so and, as she had thought, there was just about six feet in which to put her bath. The loos were installed where the original earth closets or 'long drops' were situated. Somehow the result is that an arctic gale hurtles up round the fitted mahogany seat and you are virtually in hover mode. Not conducive to a good read.

## THE PAGODA ROOM

I WAS ONCE POLITELY asked by an American visitor why we called this the Pagoda Room. Gazing mutely at the all too evident mother-of-pearl pagoda standing five feet high on the table in front of the window, and the smaller version on the table near the fire, I was somewhat fazed.

Family history is well represented in the portraits. The one which dominates the room depicts the Treasurer. Painted at the peak of his career, he is shown by the artist, Marcus Gheeraerts, holding his wand of office and wearing the robes and Order of the Garter. I would dearly have loved to meet the old man. He has a most charming face. In spite of his high office, he was never pompous and to his friends was 'Oft times merry among gentle men and fond of laughter'. Any man who was able to serve such a difficult queen and retain his head and her affection must have been worth knowing.

Queen Elizabeth is shown in a rather cruel portrait once also attributed to Gheeraerts. A fanatically vain woman, she would not have liked this portrait with its wrinkled and aged visage, from which even a ruby the size of a tomato in her hair cannot detract. She is certainly not in the first flush of youth. I am reminded of the loyal report that 'Her Majesty takes a bath twice a month whether she needs it or not'.

The painting of Charles I's children is a copy by John Stone, after the original by Van Dyck. A superb mastiff dominates the group with a small spaniel eyeing him, obviously wondering whether it's worth having a bit of a go. Underneath hang two pictures which, in the days before accuracy got in the way of a good story, were called *Rembrandt's Parents* and were

*Lime-wood carvings, the work of the Gibbons school, late 17th century, surround Liberi's* Logic between Vice and Virtue *in the Black and Yellow Bedroom*

*(opposite) The Black and Yellow Bedroom, with one of the Soho 'Grotesque' tapestries by John Vanderbank behind the bed*

said to be by their rather well-known son. Sadly, they are now described as being in the manner of Rembrandt.

There used to be a hideous overmantel in here, carved by prisoners of war in about 1916 from a tree which fell in the park. Although thoroughly praiseworthy and kindly meant as a gift for granny, somehow it did not add much to the decor and is now preserved for future generations in the guides' sitting room.

Another pair of the glorious English serpentine commodes is on view in this room. These are almost my favourite pieces in the whole house. They are of the finest quality throughout and the drawers work like silk. (I am reminded of the exhortation to a housemaid in a domestic instruction manual: 'If your drawers stick, put candle grease along the bottom edges.')

## THE BLUE SILK BEDROOM

THIS ROOM WAS originally christened 'The Purple Satin Bedroom'. Sadly, the purple satin disintegrated and the bed on which it was displayed was put into store when we arrived in 1982. My parents had always slept in a marvellous eighteenth-century bed made by Ince and Mayhew, and we decided to move it in as a replacement. Hung with scarlet and blue velvet and silk, it is one of the finest examples to be found anywhere. The posts, heavily carved with acanthus leaves and berries, proved an irresistible challenge to my father as a small boy. He climbed them regularly. 'Fine going up but absolute hell coming down' was his comment.

The bed cover was something of a discovery. Tucked at the back of one of the endless cupboards in the linen room, was a plastic wrapped bundle of filthy Jacobean-type embroidery. We sent it to the workshops at Hatfield House and in a matter of months they had cleaned it, removed the twisted Victorian brown thread from the edge of each flower and leaf, mounted the whole onto a new twill background and finished it with a handmade fringe.

The cabinet on stand which glows in the background is probably one of the rarest items in the house. Made by Pierre Gôle, cabinet maker to Louis XIV, it is *en suite* with a pair of torchères and a table. For years it loitered unrecognized outside the gent's loo on the ground floor. It took the visit of Professor Lunsingh Scheurleer from Leyden to identify it correctly. Suddenly imbued with previously unthought-of grandeur, it was first whisked to the restorers and then to the place of honour which it now occupies.

When the cabinet returned from Paul Kelaart, who works on the furniture for us, we were appalled by the dazzling array of newly gilded feet and escutcheons. Mindful of how an over-gilded piece of furniture can ruin the harmonious whole of an historic interior, we toned the gilding down. Sneakily, though, we are rather proud of its glitter and are gathering our resources prior to starting on the table and torchères.

When we stripped the Victorian treacle varnish from the walls in here, we found the residue of the original marbled decoration. In poor shape, there was not enough to make it worth keeping except for a small sample as an historical record. The technique seems to be very similar to that employed in the library at Lincoln Cathedral, which had been done by 1696, possibly within twenty years or so of when the Burghley decoration was done.

Edna Curtis, who was lady's maid to my mother, can recall this room being used by weekend guests. It is not over large and was convenient for the facilities in the passage. The temperature must have been well below freezing in winter with no heating except for the small grate in the corner. On the mantelpiece stand the same *blanc de chine* figures that were in here in 1688; all credit to 300 years of housemaids and careful dusting.

## THE BLUE SILK DRESSING ROOM

I RECALL READING the phrase 'a massy show' somewhere in an old inventory, meaning, I presume, a dazzling array of whatever. In here we have tried to achieve 'a massy show' of seventeenth- and eighteenth-century Chinese porcelain. It felt good to do it in this room because in the winter of 1990 we panelled the walls in dark blue moiré silk, which not only looks rather splendid with the paintings but also sets off the tiers of pots excellently. In addition there is a new corner chimneypiece, which replaced the ugly Victorian version; and the walls are once again marbled to match the bolection moulded fireplace in a subtle mixture of sepia, russet and dove grey.

*Kakiemon-style group of two wrestlers c.1670–85, documented in the 1688 inventory as 'Two China Boyes Wrestling'*

*The Marquetry Room, one of the rooms along the west front that were formed from the original Elizabethan long gallery. Part of the collection of 17th-century Japanese porcelain is displayed on the chimneypiece. Pieter Brueghel the Younger's* Rent Day *can be seen above the chest of drawers. To its right is Demontreuil's carving of a dead bird.*

It is a terrifying experience teetering at the top of an aluminium ladder, with your head spinning because of the height and your arms full of Ming. Simon and our daughter Miranda spent a whole day offering pieces up, rejecting certain shapes, and finally deciding on the pattern and 'line' they wanted to end up with.

A small painting situated just where you come through the door could escape your eye unless you were watching for it. Painted by Orazio Gentileschi, depicting *The Virgin and Child*, it was swapped for a telescope in the eighteenth century with Pope Clement XIV.

The story is that the ninth Earl of Exeter was in Rome and had been to the Vatican to look at the pictures, as tourists do today. Somewhere he found this little gem and approached a cardinal to enquire if His Holiness would consider parting with it. 'Absolutely not' was the response, for it was one of the Pope's most favourite paintings. Not easily discouraged, the Earl tried another tack: 'What would be the present most appreciated by His Holiness if he, the Earl, were to send him one?' 'Well,' came the reply, 'The Holy Father has always rather desired a really good telescope.' The Earl returned to England and purchased the best telescope available. He sent it to the cardinal and it was presented to the Pope, who was delighted with this unexpected and apposite gift. 'What' he asked the cardinal, 'should we send this English Protestant milord in return?' 'How about that small painting in the anteroom?' suggested the Machiavellian cardinal. The painting was wrapped and on its way to England in an instant. It would be interesting to know if the telescope remains in the Vatican, and I hope the cardinal received a hefty contribution to his favourite charity in return for his skilled manoeuvres.

There is an eighteenth-century 'zed' bed in the window embrasure. Made to resemble a sofa, it is very hard to sit on, but it has a cunning pull-out base which transforms into a webbed construction with two very wobbly bed posts, over which you draped your cloak to keep at bay the noxious night air. It was made locally in Stamford by a man called Robert Tymperon, presumably for valets or lady's maids who needed to remain within call during the night. However, one false move and the whole post business would collapse and smite you unconscious.

## THE FIRST GEORGE ROOM

THE FIFTH EARL of Exeter was beguiled by all things Italian, despite his dealings with a brilliant but excitable native of Naples, Antonio Verrio (1630–1707), who was employed at Burghley in the years 1686–97.

Antonio was married at fifteen in his own city but abandoned his wife to come to England as the protegé of Ralph Montagu (the fifth Earl's cousin) in 1672. He worked for Charles II at Windsor but the change of regime in 1685 meant he was out of a job. Forced by circumstances to seek employment in the great houses of Protestant noblemen, he began to work for the fifth Earl on a suite of rooms occupying the south range of Burghley – the Great State Rooms. We have no real idea why these rooms were called the George Rooms. Maybe after the saint who then failed to appear in any of the designs, or maybe after the St George Hall at Windsor where Verrio had worked for King Charles. Who knows?

Verrio was an extraordinarily difficult character to manage. Fiery and unpredictable, he ground down the wretched Culpepper Tanner who, as the Earl's secretary, had to deal with him. As far as we can judge from the records he was at odds with almost everyone in the house while he was occupied painting the south facing rooms. He had a keen appreciation of the naked female form and wreaked havoc among the serving girls, quarrelling along the way with the cook, whose visage was portrayed on one ceiling cast in the role of 'Plenty' – improved by the addition of four extra breasts, no doubt to her everlasting rage.

The artist charged the fifth Earl something between £50 and £150 for painting this room and the Jewel Closet which leads off it. But he was hopeless with money and spent every penny as soon as he had it, sometimes even before he had it. When in funds, he stayed at the George Hotel in Stamford. A bill exists for '26 bottles of red port and 2 of sherrey' and from the entry '26 empty Botls: 5/–' it seems that most of them were broken in the jollification. From the final item: 'Yourself; Bed and Bread' he obviously did not make it home again after dinner. When money ran out, Verrio stayed in a wayside tavern of no reputation until the next payday.

Verrio worked with the assistance of a gilder, René Cousin, and an architectural artist called Alexandre Souville. Antonio's forte was people; the flying gods and goddesses, mythological figures and even his self-portrait are of staggering quality. We should, perhaps, forgive him, there-

*Queen Elizabeth I after Marcus Gheeraerts*

*(opposite) 'Queen Elizabeth's Bedroom' – although she never used it. The 17th-century state bed has been fully restored. The magnificent Gobelins tapestries purchased by the 5th Earl are included in the 1688 inventory*

fore, for being such a pain to deal with, and even overlook his passion for boots and shoes, bought in such quantity as to plunge him into debt. He was finally imprisoned for non-payment of bills, having been pursued doggedly for six years by two carpenters from London.

In the Earl's absence, Culpepper Tanner did a good job of keeping an eye on Verrio to make sure he did not dash off to the fleshpots of London when he was supposed to be working. This rather cramped his style and meant he felt trapped at Burghley. It was perhaps not all that surprising therefore that Verrio accepted with alacrity the invitation to go and paint a ceiling or two for 'My Lord Devon' at Chatsworth.

When Verrio went to Chatsworth, part of his lifestyle improved. For example, there he had wheels on his scaffolding; but he was expected to find the 'Dyett' for himself and his horse out of his salary, whereas at Burghley it was an extra perk. He soon returned here and continued beautifying room after room until for some reason, probably lack of wages, he was deserted by his gilder, and was forced to complete the final ceiling of the Hell Staircase virtually on his own. This was no easy task. He had to lie on a rudimentary 'fleake' or tower scaffolding about sixty feet from the ground, or was suspended on a cradle called a 'craike', and had to get the perspective right so that it appeared correct from the ground floor. There are not many artists who can boast a talent like that. There is a portrait at Beningbrough Hall, Yorkshire, of him in old age inscribed 'Ecco Antonio O' il povero Verrio'.

For all his faults Verrio's work has remained as the great glory of the house and if you ask a cross section of youngsters what they remember about their visit here they will usually reply: 'All those gentlemen and ladies with nothing on, painted on the ceilings.'

This first George room is intimate enough to accept happily a quantity of small paintings. An exquisite panel picture hangs on the left just as you go in. Painted by a man with the memorable name of 'Il Bastorolo', this was in an appalling state when we arrived, with the paint actually falling onto the floor. Alec Cobbe rescued it just in time and it now glows cheerfully, conserved for the future.

The dramatic painting over the fireplace of *The Boy David* was attributed for many years to a second-rate follower of Andrea Del Sarto. When Alec Cobbe began the painstaking task of removing several generations of overpaint, he was intrigued by the pentimento or drawing that showed through the fragile remaining original pigments. We had various complex photographic tests carried out on the painting and became more and more convinced that here was either the hand of the master or the hand of a gifted studio assistant. Another version of this painting exists, now in the Pitti Palace in Florence, which for many years has been accepted as the original with ours a poor copy. We sent the results of the tests and the photographs to the curators at the Pitti Palace but not a squeak have we heard. One of the most abiding irritants is the inability of Italian museums to reply to letters. In this instance they are perhaps worried that the Burghley picture is the original, but at the very least it would be good to compare the results of tests.

I was once recounting this long and involved tale to a large audience at a lecture in San Francisco. Suddenly there was a polite cough and a tall distinguished gentleman in the second row stood up and said 'Excuse me Ma'am but my name is Del Sarto'. My mouth fell open and all I could think of to say was 'Do you paint much?' Quite a coincidence.

Burghley is well known for having the best and most numerous collection of silver fireplaces in the country and in here is the first example encountered on the tour. Every year before we open the house, devoted scrubbing and polishing with toothbrushes is necessary to bring the fireplaces up to scratch, but from then on they are simply rubbed up with a silver cloth to maintain their appearance through the season. There was a radio programme a few years ago in which an interviewer discussed the fireplaces with an 'expert'. This man came out with the astonishing information that the Burghley examples were totally useless because when a fire was lit they would melt.

## THE JEWEL CLOSET

WE PRESUME THAT the First George Room was used as a dressing room, in which case the little closet leading off it could have been used either as a small devotional chamber, with perhaps a prie-dieu and a crucifix, or as a toilette with a dressing table, washbasin and close stool. I rather hope it was used for the former purpose as one of the greatest religious paintings in the house, *Our Lord blessing the Bread and Wine* by Carlo Dolci, hangs in here now, and looks quite at home.

The vivid apple green damask with which my grandmother covered the walls fell to pieces, largely because of the sun which streams into all

*William Cecil, Lord Burghley, by Marcus Gheeraerts*

*(opposite) The Pagoda Room contains some notable portraits and two of a set of fine 18th-century English serpentine mahogany commodes*

these south-facing rooms. Sadly the shade of apple green was one of those now unobtainable except at the horrendous cost of a special dye run and so we hung the walls with primrose yellow silk.

The room is so tiny (about eight feet square) that there is only a table and stool in it. On either side of the table stand two large snake-handled maiolica vases, dated 1670, and brought back here by the fifth Earl from one of his Italian marauds. It always amazes me that these fragile works of art arrived home in one piece. Perhaps the necessarily slow pace of the transport – ox-carts – had something to do with their survival.

Historically, jewels were housed in the cupboard set into the wall, thereby giving this room its name. As a small child I would gaze fascinatedly at this 'Cabinet of Curiosities', what the Germans and Austrians call a Kunstkammer. There was an absorbing collection of objects, including pieces of coral, shells, odd bits of bone, an old silk hankie (property of Charles I and no doubt the very one used to blow his nose on the scaffold), 'Billies and Charlies', those fake ancient coins purporting to be Roman found near the Thames, agate dishes, and wonderful serpentine-handled knives and forks. Gold and enamelled pocket watches hung from hooks on the shelves, amber statues of saints and silver-gilt mounted dishes jostled for space, while, most precious of all, a little enamelled Elizabethan horse, set with rubies and pearls that might have hung from a silken girdle at the court of the Virgin Queen herself, dazzled the gaze as it swung trembling to the vibration of our footsteps.

What a treasure trove. The collection was brought to Burghley by the wife of the fifth Earl as part of her inheritance from her mother, the Countess of Devonshire. It was tucked away in this cupboard from 1690 to 1956, when sadly it was stored away in bakers' trays, and buried under layers of sawdust for security reasons. This collection, known as The Countess's Gems, has been one of our most exciting discoveries (see p.66) and in 1989 was put on show to the public for the first time. It subsequently travelled to New York where it was displayed at the Cooper Hewitt Museum.

*(opposite) Chinese porcelain of the 17th and 18th centuries displayed in the Blue Silk Dressing Room*

*Marquetry cabinet by Pierre Gôle*

*(opposite) The Blue Silk Bedroom has a rare French marquetry cabinet by Pierre Gôle, 1665*

**Virgin and Child Resting** *by Orazio Gentileschi, in the Blue Silk Dressing Room, originally belonged to Pope Clement XIV, who swapped it for a telescope*

*(opposite) The First George Room. The first of the great State Rooms on the south side of the house, with one of Verrio's dramatic ceilings*

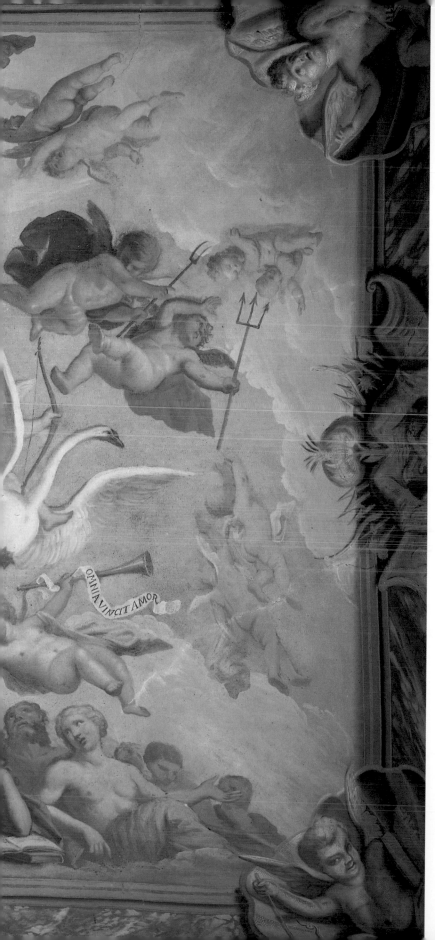

OMNIA VINCIT AMOR

*Ceiling by Antonio Verrio in the Jewel Closet*

*(overleaf left) The Second George Room, used by Queen Victoria and Prince Albert. The bed, made in 1791, has been restored. The tapestries are by John Vanderbank*

*(overleaf right) The south wall of the Second George Room*

*Rock-crystal bottle set with rubies and emeralds, Mughal, 17th century. This is documented in the 1690 Deed of Gift*

*Perfume bottle, agate, mounted in silver-gilt and set with turquoises and rubies, 1540. Documented in the 1690 Deed of Gift*

*Verrio's ceiling for the Second George Room depicting various gods and goddesses, for which he was paid £200*

SIC VIRTVS
EVEHIT
ARDENS ( HONOR
PVLCHERRIMA
MERCES IPSE SIBI

*The Fourth George Room with the marquetry table and 17th-century cabinet on stand*

*(opposite) The Third George Room. Luca Giordano's* The Death of Seneca, *is the large painting on the left, and one of Giuseppe Recco's flowerpieces is to the left of the fireplace*

*Elizabethan wall painting revealed behind the panelling in the Fourth George Room*

## THE SECOND GEORGE ROOM

OWING TO THE OUTBREAK of yachts and racehorses which decimated the family fortunes during the nineteenth century Burghley escaped the scourge of Victorian improvements which have, in an architectural sense, spoiled many of Britain's great houses.

One of the squanderers was the second Marquess. He and his wife, as we have seen, were not particularly popular, but in spite of their various personal shortcomings, they managed to persuade Queen Victoria and Prince Albert to come to stay for the weekend when the Prince stood sponsor to Lady Victoria Cecil at her christening in 1844. The royal couple slept in this bedroom.

According to an account written by a member of the family at the time, the whole weekend was a hectic affair. Lord Exeter went to greet the royal couple on their journey through Northamptonshire. Having made his mark there, he then galloped back to Burghley, changed into tidy clothes and was on hand to greet the Queen as she stepped out of the coach.

That evening there was no major entertainment laid on as the visitors were fatigued. They slept in the specially refurbished state bed, made by Newton and Fell for 3,000 guineas in 1791. The bed belonged originally to the tenth Countess, who used to receive the daughters of the gentry sitting propped with cushions on her new and expensive furniture 'appropriately dressed for chocolate'. When the bed was new it had 'cantoons', great swags of fabric sweeping down on either side of the foot of the tester, and fastened onto posts which were inserted into moveable bases so that you could choose whether to have the 'cantoons' like wings on either side or level with the bed foot. By the time Queen Victoria came, the bed had been topped with a frightful pair of gilded doves, swags of unlikely flowers and a large new base with head and foot boards inserted under the canopy. Everything that the Queen was likely to set eyes on was gilded. Perfectly good, honest mahogany chairs were gilded to within an inch of their lives for the royal couple's delight; everything glittered.

*(overleaf) The Heaven Room, described as Verrio's masterpiece. Verrio depicted himself seated by a pillar, without his wig, in the Cyclops's forge at the end of the room.*

The next morning the christening took place in the Chapel. It was not without incident. The Bishop of Peterborough took the service, but he arrived rather under the influence of sherry which he had taken to calm his nerves. In addition he had forgotten his glasses, which meant he had to guess how the wording went. He began the christening first of all without the Queen, then without the baby. Finally the deed was done and the party went outside for a tree-planting ceremony. Queen Victoria was quite small and the spade that she was given was large and heavy. When it became obvious that she was unable to lift it, a wooden child's spade from the sandpit was sent for and she completed the task with that. This spade, elevated in status by having been touched by the royal glove, now graces a chair beside the bed for visitors to puzzle over. The tree planted by Queen Victoria, as well as the one planted by Prince Albert, can be seen from the window of this room.

That evening there was an enormous banquet in the Great Hall. Prince Albert made a speech and gave the Marquess a portrait as a keepsake. With some relief on both sides the jollifications ended the next day and the royal party went back to London. Not, however, before the Queen had let it be known to one of her ladies-in-waiting that she 'detested Lady Exeter for her overwhelming odour of sanctity and because she found her a great bore'.

Refurbishing this room was one of our first priorities and when we were lucky enough to receive the necessary financial support from the Cotton Trust, it went ahead with all speed. Eugene Shortall, who had already helped us with the refurbishment of Queen Elizabeth's bed, arranged for silk to be dyed to match the original velvet, sadly unobtainable nowadays. He had the white satin under the canopy made specially and also made curtains to the only design we had – a drawing of the room when the Queen came. We could not take the pattern from what was left as all we had were one or two tragic bits of frayed material. Thankfully, many of the original braids and tassels were in good enough order to be cleaned and re-used. The expense of trying to recreate these intricate decorations would have been prohibitive.

The Vanderbank tapestries were washed and rehung, and the beautiful new curtains protected from the touch of the appreciative public by scarlet net, bought in the John Lewis department store in Peterborough. When the interested and chatty sales lady was measuring out the required length she said to me, 'Ooh, lovely colour, are you going dancing?'

The fireplace is of a splendid liver-colour marble and, unusually, mounted with gilt bronze. It was made to a design by Piranesi and ordered for this room by the ninth Earl during his travels in Italy. There are eight boxwood carvings of mythological figures and ancient roman Caesars on the mantelshelf above. These are very rare and interesting and were bought in the seventeenth century by the fifth Earl in Italy. They are mentioned in our 1688 inventory. Of sublime quality, they are a delight.

Above the fireplace hangs a painting by the Revd Dr Peters. He was religious instructor to the young Princess Victoria and had a tendency to portray his subjects (always worthy) on the way up or on the way down, or, as in this case, suspended in mid air, entitled *Soul of a young girl ascending to Heaven*.

The chest of drawers on the opposing wall is most probably a product of the workshops of Ince and Mayhew, because the triple loop design, or *guilloche*, as seen in the satinwood marquetry inlay to the top, is one of their favourites.

The extraordinary figure of an ostrich which stands here is a real oddity. Made from an actual ostrich egg mounted with a Meissen porcelain head and neck, and garnished with silver gilt wings and legs, it is certainly not to everyone's taste. However, our local boy-scout troop had a collection and raised £77 for its restoration. I had a crazy conversation with the man in a Bond Street jeweller's shop when I asked him if his company could mend two wonky legs on an antique ostrich.

## THE THIRD GEORGE ROOM

QUEEN VICTORIA used this room as her private sitting room when she visited Burghley in 1844. It must have been really quite gloomy if the colour of the walls when we came was the same as in her day. The walls were hung in a dismal dark shade of maroon silk damask; a real beast of a colour as a backdrop to Italian paintings. Of course it is easy to blame all this on the Edwardians as the colour was chic at the beginning of the century, but maybe they were copying what was there before. It is not often that we are grateful for floods, but when water came in through the ceiling of this room in 1983 it provided an excellent excuse to redecorate. It was not just the water which caused damage to the walls. There is a curious trap or vent for one of the few chimneys in regular use

tucked into one of the walls. Capability Brown can be blamed for the problems we have suffered with this one; always smoking and in fact frequently on fire, it made our lives a misery. The stalwart British public stumbled through here, before it was fixed, unable to see anything at all and with tears running down their faces, and emerged at the end of their tour totally kippered. Mr Brown had underestimated the problems that faulty design and the inclusion in the flue of an old oak beam could cause. The walls have been recovered and the chimney lined, so things are a touch more normal now.

Capability Brown designed various chimneys at Burghley, which in some cases are incorporated in the balustrading around the roof. It should also be mentioned that he replaced almost all the Elizabethan diamond-paned glass and created gothic-arched windows, when he was employed by the ninth Earl in the years 1756–79.

*Part of the 6th Marquess's collection of Chinese snuff bottles*

*(opposite) Pietra-dura cabinet in the Heaven Room given to the 5th Earl as a gift by Cosimo de' Medici*

The two large document or map chests which are *en suite* with the encoignures are fun because they are made from seventeenth-century marquetry cunningly incorporated in newer carcases by Ince and Mayhew in the eighteenth century. However, putting old and new timber together can give rise to problems. One day there was a tour going through this room when there was a noise like an air rifle and a locked door on one of the chests burst open. All was evidently not well. We asked John Bly, known to viewers of British television by his frequent appearances on programmes to do with antiques, and who also restores furniture for us, to have a look. He deduced that the new and old timber were acting against one another and causing stresses which had caused the door to buckle. He took away the doors from both chests and straightened them out in his workshop.

A month or so later he and I, both looking a trifle scruffy in jeans and jerseys, were hard at work fixing the hinges. We could hear the distant tones of an approaching tour group and so we speeded up. As luck would have it, we put the right-hand door on the left-hand cabinet, and were to be seen crawling behind the furniture in the furthest reaches of the room in order not to be noticed as the party entered. 'And here Ladies and Gentlemen, as a real treat, is someone I'm sure you will recognize … John Bly.' Poor John had to stand up before his fans and cope with the situation, trying to explain we were not playing bears behind the sofa but restoring two important commodes.

A well-known manufacturer of eighteenth-century marble fireplaces, Dr Bossi, is represented in this room. In the years 1785–98 he perfected a technique of inlaying marble paste into marble fireplaces and tables in the style of Robert Adam. He was reputed to have worked in Dublin among other places and was famous for the subtlety of his craftsmanship. It is said that on his deathbed his son came to him and begged him for the secret of his coloured pastes. 'Father, you are dying,' he said, 'please tell me how you achieve these wonderful effects.' 'No' said his father and died. So that was that.

Standing on the Bossi-work fireplace is a marble head of Medusa. The snakes forming her hair are horribly realistic and slightly over lifesize. It is a commanding piece and not one you would want in your sitting room. It was made by Nollekens, one of the best-known suppliers of sculpture to the gentry on the Grand Tour in the eighteenth century; it is one of several works by him in the house.

On the east and west walls there are two huge paintings by Luca Giordano who was much patronized by the fifth Earl when he visited Florence. The one on the left shows Seneca, tutor to the young Nero, committing suicide by bleeding to death rather than see his instructions ignored. This picture has an almost exact duplicate in the Palacio Real in Madrid, except that in the Spanish version, instead of the small and embarrassed dog who has obviously misbehaved just out of frame, there is a pile of books; much more reliable. Flanking the fireplace, the two large flowerpieces, also bought by the fifth Earl, are by the Neapolitan artist Giuseppe Recco and were shown at the Royal Academy in 1981.

Below the window stands a much less elevated example of scagliola work than the fireplace. This table has been carefully attacked by visitors who find a fascination in removing pieces of the coloured material with their fingernails.

## THE FOURTH GEORGE ROOM

IF WE WERE TO acknowledge a ghost at Burghley, this is the room in which he would belong. Firstly, this is because of a tale told to me by an ex-guide to the house some years ago: 'I was walking through the rooms closing up for the night; it was about ten minutes to six. I opened the door into the Fourth George and a very cross male voice said, just by my shoulder, "Oh, a pox on it".' Obviously a spectral inhabitant who thought he was free of pesky visitors for the day. Secondly, I had the impression one day of a tall male figure dressed in black beside the fireplace; a blink and it was gone, but the feeling remains that he was there.

*(overleaf left) The Hell Staircase, installed in 1786 by the 9th Earl on the cantilever principal, is pleasantly airy in contrast to Verrio's dark scenes of Hell on the ceiling and the somewhat gloomy walls painted by Thomas Stothard in 1802*

*(overleaf right) The Great Hall, considerably altered since its original use in the 16th century for feasting and dancing. The double hammer-beam construction of the room is comparable to Middle Temple hall built in 1562. The fireplace and the minstrels' gallery date from the late 18th century*

The complex marquetry table in the middle of the room has a story to tell. Originally square, not round, it probably originated in Germany or Holland in about 1590. The fine interlaced strapwork, once dyed green, is a testament to its original brilliance. Subsequently, fashions changed and a large round table was needed for this room. Can we blame the alteration that ensued on Queen Victoria's visit? Oh, I do hope so. Anyhow, the table was enlarged and made circular. It was done as well as possible; to the casual glance it is all of a piece, until you look at the base which, formed from a series of arcaded motifs, bears little resemblance to sixteenth-century design and would even cause puzzlement in the twentieth century. It remains a mysterious object.

I have to mention the role of the expert in a house such as this. It can happen that a faulty attribution by some 'expert', who quite often has not actually examined a picture, can blight the future of that painting for a generation. No person faced with organizing an exhibition, of the paintings of Gentileschi for example, could safely go against the top man or woman in that field, even though this person may not have seen the picture. And when experts do come to the house, on a dark November day and, without a torch, view from the top rung of a tottering ladder a picture requiring urgent cleaning, it is rare to hear them say, 'In all honesty I don't know who painted this.' It seems to be necessary to reach a conclusion, even though the commercial value of the article in question may vary, depending on the verdict, by many thousands of pounds. I recall laughing with the Duchess of Devonshire a few years ago as she energetically consigned a letter from an art expert to the bin. 'Really,' she said, 'if I took notice of every daft attribution of the pictures at Chatsworth, we'd have gone bankrupt paying for the gold leaf to re-do the labels.'

I am enormously lucky that, due to my job with Sotheby's, I can call on a number of talented advisers, and indeed would not have survived the last few years without their help. How do people manage historic houses without assistance such as this? We are immensely fortunate in having John Somerville as our honorary keeper of pictures. He is a great believer in getting other skilled advisers to the house and consulting with them. It is all the more puzzling therefore that books continue to be written about pictures which the author has never bothered to see or last examined under layers of grime in bad light in the 1960s. I am afraid it all makes you a trifle cynical.

The strange cabinet on stand at the back of this room is worth a close look, if only to marvel firstly at the skill of the man who made it in Antwerp in about 1685, and secondly at the skill of the restorer who made it look so good in 1989. The wooden carcase is veneered with a fine layer of blonde tortoiseshell inset with carved battle scenes executed in pewter, copper and mother of pearl. Prior to its restoration, large sections of pewter were missing or extremely faint, the tortoiseshell was a uniform shade of dull brown, and the door to the central cupboard was hanging off.

I went to visit the cabinet in 'hospital' at the London workshop of one of our furniture restorers, David Hordern. His workshop was a joy, full of dedicated young craftsmen each allocated a particular 'patient' to care for. The cabinet was stripped down and, with its drawers removed, it was possible to be appalled at the 'orange box' approach of the original maker where he thought he could get away with it. Scrappy bits of softwood were tacked together any-old-how, ready to receive the glamorous coating of inlay and veneer. Enough of the original outline of the pewter scenes was discernible for them to be re-engraved. The replacement plaques were cut and etched so finely that I defy anyone to tell them from the originals.

We are walking the narrow tightrope between 'conservation' and 'restoration' all the time. It is a tough decision to correct the ravages of woodworm on a piece without perhaps gilding its little handles. Hard too to turn your back on the possibility of once more making an object the focus of attention by not replacing plaques of silver or gilt or ivory. Everyone knows that the value of an item can be affected by recent restoration, but as we hope not to have to sell anything, that consideration does not apply. However, conscious that we will be judged by history for mistakes we make, we are always a little nervous when an object goes to be repaired. It is, though, such fun when it comes home all dulled up, goes back into its allotted space and GLOWS.

The pietra-dura table in the window is rather special. It is possible really to admire the Florentine brilliance of the many coloured hardstones employed in the pattern. Once again, I am full of admiration for the packing and shipping that brought it safely to Stamford before the end of the seventeenth century. In the eighteenth century, marble statues were occasionally packed in crates, lined with bushy branches. This is recorded at Holkham Hall in Norfolk, where the seeds from the ilex trees

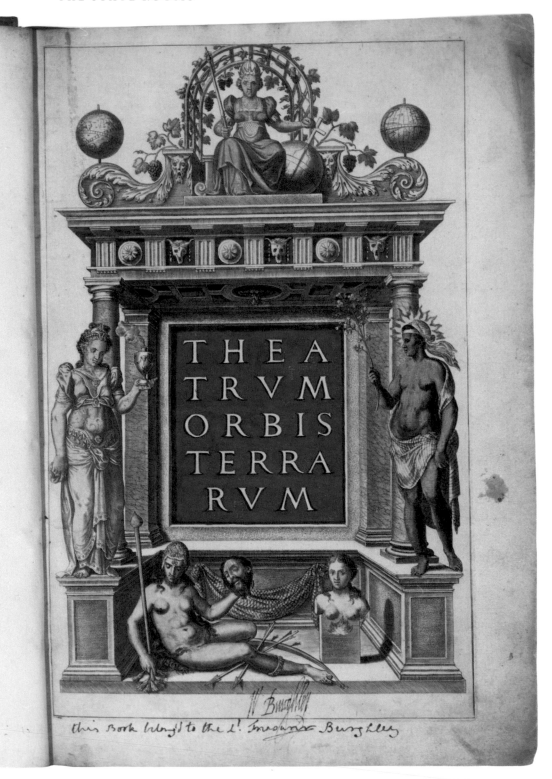

THEA
TRVM
ORBIS
TERRA
RVM

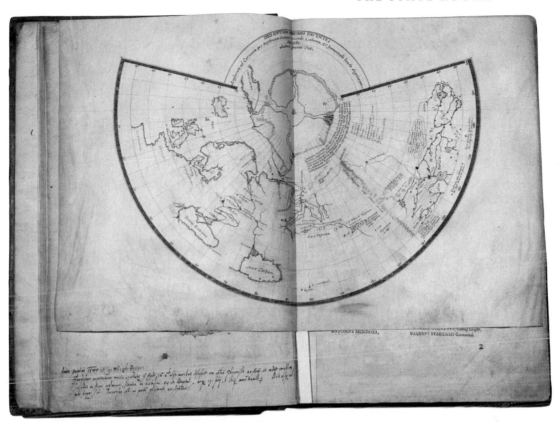

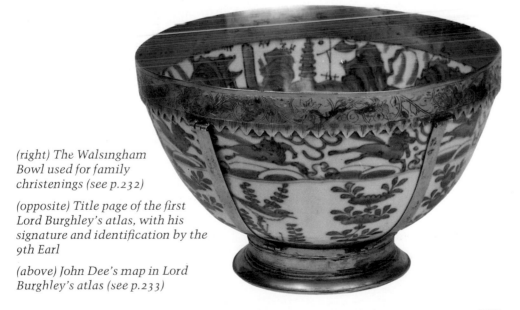

*(right) The Walsingham Bowl used for family christenings (see p.232)*

*(opposite) Title page of the first Lord Burghley's atlas, with his signature and identification by the 9th Earl*

*(above) John Dee's map in Lord Burghley's atlas (see p.233)*

which cushioned the marble figure of 'Diana' when she was 'brought up from Woolwich' in a box, sprouted and grew into the avenue still at Holkham today. At least that is the story and who wants to disbelieve it?

In 1987 we had a bonus when a workman stripping off the wooden panelling from above the windows in this room discovered the traces of the original Elizabethan fresco. It presumably ran the length of the gallery which was divided up to create these state apartments in the seventeenth century. The oak panelling was reinstated, but the fresco was photographed before it was hidden from view once again.

## THE HEAVEN ROOM

THIS HAS BEEN CALLED Antonio Verrio's masterpiece and is decorated with 'scenes of Gods and Goddesses disporting themselves as Gods and Goddesses are wont to do'. It was so described by a nineteenth-century cleric called in to catalogue the State Rooms. His powers of description were obviously wearing a trifle thin by the time he reached this room.

It was a major undertaking, taking seventy-five weeks to finish a room measuring thirty-nine feet by twenty-seven, for a fee of £500. Converted roughly into its modern equivalent the fee would seem generous – somewhere in the high tens of thousands of pounds. Taken out of this, however, was the keep for Verrio and his assistants, the fodder for his horse, the paints and gold leaf, brushes, turpentine and so on. This was the room which caused the greatest rows between the artist and his employer. The fifth Earl became involved, unusually, in a personal battle, calling Verrio an 'impudent dogg'. Verrio retorted that he had no time to work for the Earl and felt justified in delegating the figure painting for which he alone was responsible.

From time to time we use this room for entertainment. Lit with candles, the figures on the walls and ceilings seem to move. The colours glow where the light catches, and Horace Walpole's comment about a similar work by Verrio at Chatsworth appears apposite: 'It seems as if Mrs Holman [a noted society hostess] had been in Heaven and invited everyone she knew.'

My father's collection of snuff bottles is displayed in front of the windows in glass-topped cabinets. They were on display in vertical cases in the Great Hall before, but a lady fainted against them and every single bottle fell over with a deafening crash. Miraculously only two were chipped, but it was obviously not an ideal way to show them.

A curious history is attached to these charming little objects. There was a Welsh missionary called Doctor Martin who worked in China until he retired in 1952. He must have held a good position, probably at court at some time, because he acquired, along with three hundred other snuff bottles, nine eighteenth-century Imperial ivory ones made for the Emperor, which are unlikely to have been offered on the open market and, as a man of the cloth, presumably he was not dealing in stolen goods.

When Doctor Martin returned to Britain upon his retirement, he needed money and decided to sell his collection. He rang a well-known London dealer. A very smooth young man answered the telephone and, in reply to the Doctor's enquiry, stated that it was most unlikely that they would have an expert available to inspect the collection in Wales in the foreseeable future and was generally so unhelpful that Doctor Martin rang his solicitor. 'Find me someone who will buy the entire collection; I don't want it to go to auction or have it split up.' As luck would have it, the same man was my father's solicitor. Knowing nothing about snuff bottles, my father nonetheless was sufficiently intrigued and impressed by what he learnt about the collection to go to Wales and buy the lot.

It could not have been a better investment. My father paid the 1952 market price, about £1500. Nowadays a single bottle can cost as much as that at the bottom end of the market. It is recognized as one of the best private collections in Europe and has been fully catalogued by Robert Kleiner, prior to being exhibited in America in 1989.

I remember my father returning from Wales in his green Bentley when we lived down in Sussex, the boot and seats crammed with cardboard boxes filled with smaller boxes. He and Doctor Martin had got on very well together but the hunt for all the pieces had been a nightmare. In the medicine cupboard, under the stairs, in the kitchen – the old man could not quite remember where he had put them all. During the search, Papa found a lovely, amber-coloured bottle made from glass with Chinese horsemen painted galloping round inside. He put it on one side and gave it to me when he got home. I loved it dearly and for all my childhood it lived in my toy box, to be taken out and admired on special occasions. I gave it back to him when I got married, and it is now in the cabinet with all the others.

Against the west wall is a superb hard-stone decorated cabinet on stand. It was given by Cosimo de' Medici to the fifth Earl of Exeter as a gift. These so-called tabernacle cabinets were used during the seventeenth and eighteenth centuries to contain all the small bibelots and treasures that were too valuable to leave out unprotected. This one is unusual as it combines marquetry and hard-stone work. It is more common to see the space between drawers and cupboards left plain in ebonized wood.

The seventeenth century is renowned for the tulip mania which swept Europe, sometimes bankrupting families and estates. It is not surprising, therefore, that the tulip flower plays a prominent part in the design of this cabinet. It is a relief that the Earl was not lured to the bulb dealers of Holland, instead of buying rather more lasting treasures in Italy and elsewhere.

## THE HELL STAIRCASE

THE CEILING HERE was the last work carried out for the fifth Earl of Exeter by Antonio Verrio. By the time he made this contract Verrio was heavily in debt, constantly being dunned for money he did not possess, and unable to keep his assistants, who drifted away to more financially secure projects.

The ceiling was painted between October 1696 and September 1697. He did the work with no gilded enrichment, and he was contracted to complete it for the sum of £200. It must have been a miserable time for Verrio. Hell is not the most cheerful subject to portray, nor the inhabitants of its nether regions, called into being by a tormented imagination. He must have been cold, poor, aging and lonely, and it is not surprising that the moment it was done he escaped to work for the King, leaving local trades people with unpaid bills well over the amount he had earned for the work.

As far as we know, the walls remained blank until an artist called Thomas Stothard painted them in 1802. You wish he hadn't. He obviously lacked experience in observing the female form unclothed, and his women writhe round the walls afflicted with every known disability of the spinal column; orthopaedic surgeons could write award-winning theses on the women in here. It is a mercy that, owing to the appalling lighting, it is almost impossible to see the full effect of the humps. One day, I suppose, we shall be forced to clean the walls, but I cannot bear to think about the horror that will spring to the eye and mesmerize the luckless visitor.

The seemingly-unsupported flights of stairs rise up on either side leaving a space in the middle which is very hard to furnish satisfactorily. We took the weighty decision to put all the marble sarcophagi, busts, figures of children and assorted Caesars' heads in here, arranged on tables with hardstone tops and freestanding like an eighteenth-century sculpture gallery. It sort of works, but I would love to know what items were intended for this space when the stairs were altered in the late eighteenth century by the tenth Earl, after a design by Robert Adam.

The echoes which accompany unfurnished areas are precious. Whistling in here is one of the most satisfactory pastimes. My Aunt Romayne was rocketed at school for whistling and so was I (a psalm written out by hand twenty times for 'whistling in the corridor like an errand boy'); however, when one is unable to play an instrument it has to do. The second Marquess obviously liked the empty sound too. He put his new musical box at the bottom of the stairs. An egocentric affair, it is inlaid with the family coat of arms, stands on a table specially adapted to take the hefty brass cylinders and has the bells organized so that they are bashed by brass bees. The cylinder we have in use at the moment is stirringly patriotic, playing 'Rule Britannia' and the National Anthem. Musical evenings in 1840 must have been a riot ...

When I first came to Burghley in the 1950s, it was considered a daring game to 'haunt' the visitors in here. There was a hideous walnut rocking chair belonging to my mother which rocked very nicely when a piece of fishing line was attached to the back. As children, my cousins and I would hide behind the pillars and in the middle of the guide's talk gently manipulate the chair. Hankies crammed in our mouths to stop the inevitable explosion of mirth at the sight of the horrified visitors' faces, we were much cast down when one of the guides remarked acidly: 'Come out from behind that pillar Lady Victoria, I can see your shoe.'

## THE GREAT HALL

NOT MANY OF Britain's great houses can boast that a fire engine was parked in their banqueting hall, but this is exactly what happened at Burghley during the latter years of the seventeenth century. At that time it was no longer the fashion to entertain on a grand scale; smaller select dinners in the family dining room were more usual. The only reason we know about the fire engine is through the 1688 inventory, which states that the room was full of 'servants' lumber', 'trunks', the fire engine and twenty-four buckets. Probably the very latest design, sprouting pumps, pistons and goodness knows what (or even Watt) else.

Before the seventeenth century, we can only surmise that this great hall was used in the traditional way for feasting and dancing. The 1688 inventory mentions 'a cedar raille', which might have been the front of a dais where the host and hostess would sit, and perhaps some good Elizabethan furniture would have been in use such as refectory tables, benches, plain monastic pieces, as well as a selection of buffets, court cupboards and so on.

Once the fifth Earl started on his avowed intent to 'modernize' the house and brought home his dreams of Italian furniture, French tables, Dutch chairs and other seventeenth-century articles, there was no longer any need for the Tudor remnants nor probably for the Great Hall either, and the room and its contents slid out of favour.

When the northwest wing was demolished in 1765, because Capability Brown said it got in the way of the view, the library which it contained became homeless. Thousands of rare and fragile books must have been piled in tottering heaps on the floor of the great hall for the best part of twenty years. The decision was finally made to build new cases and at the same time indulge in a little medieval nostalgia by putting in a minstrels' gallery. The fireplace was also radically altered. The hall is now, because of these changes, a rather unsatisfactory shape. About sixty feet high, it deserves greater width and length to improve the proportions. The floor has also been changed; once of good Ketton stone, now it is of polished wood, better for dancing on and a trifle warmer.

From that time to this I wonder if anyone ever read those books. From the accumulated beetles, worm, outbreaks of mould and general wildlife galloping around on the shelves prior to the huge book-conservation project that we began in 1987, I would think it unlikely.

In 1957 my father sold some rare maps and herbals from the collection, not realizing that together these books were unusual: a seventeenth-century gentleman's library. There are books by John Dee, magician, necromancer and Elizabethan geographer (see also p.233), and others with the book plate of William Bathon. This kept us guessing for a bit, until we were told it was Archbishop Laud who, as Bishop of Bath and Wells, used this title. That we have a smattering of Elizabethan books left, including Lord Burghley's atlas, is to me a delight.

This particular atlas gave rise to an enormous misunderstanding between myself and a Japanese professor, who arrived unannounced one day when Simon and I had just walked in through the front door after a long and tiring flight across the Atlantic. We were at that particularly disjointed and dotty stage where you know that you should go to bed but the desk is piled high with mail waiting to be dealt with. We were halfway down the heap when the professor arrived and asked to see me.

The combination of the words 'professor', 'Japan' and 'would like to see you', could mean only one thing; a porcelain expert had come all this way to inspect the Japanese pots. I swept down to greet him, he smiled and bowed politely and together we advanced on the porcelain store. Talking merrily the while, hoping I was not sounding as ga-ga as I felt, we slowly progressed until it dawned on me that all was not well. He should have been excited, inquisitive and thrilled by the treasures I was showing him, but there was no such reaction. Where was the fascinated smile and 'wah', which is the language of oriental ceramicists? There was nothing except the ever-polite smile. After a while I summoned up my courage and asked him why he had come. Daylight shone as he murmured, grateful for the least pause in the diatribe about porcelain, something about 'the Atras'. Poor man, he had come all the way from Nagoya to see Lord Burghley's atlas, and I had assumed so stupidly that he was interested in pots. He turned out to be a world authority on Ortelius, the man who made the maps in the atlas circa 1574. What was even more amazing was that he lectured on Ortelius, who was Dutch, to Italians, in English!

During its lifetime the Great Hall has seen many exhibitions. When my parents were alive they regularly showed such things as historic costumes, and even my wedding dress, which surprisingly proved rather successful. When we put the silver collection on show, most of it was in here, secured in a plate-glass house specially erected in the centre of the room. Now that we have a special exhibition room over the shop, we no longer need this space.

The Great Hall is now empty except for ten superb seventeenth-century walnut chairs from the Doge's palace in Venice, which are

197

around the walls, and, in pride of place, the enormous silver wine cooler, five feet long and three feet high, made in 1710 by Philip Rollos. Weighing over 3000 troy ounces, it is second only in size to the one in the Hermitage which Garrard and Company are copying for an American millionaire. Once a year, for the Horse Trials cocktail party, we use our wine cooler, filled with large blocks of ice and champagne bottles. It looks wonderful; really vulgar.

## THE ATHLETICS TROPHY CORRIDOR

IN THE CORRIDOR outside the Great Hall, there are various items celebrating my father's athletic career. There are photographs, a painting of him in a Cambridge blue dressing gown and two cabinets mounted on the wall containing medals, trophies, his running vest with the number 444 on the chest, a rather dashing pair of silk shorts and a tiny pair of the lightest handmade running shoes you can imagine. The medals include his 1928 gold medal and the silver medal he won in the 4 × 400 metres at the 1932 Olympics.

Down the passage you will notice that among all the photographs of sporting events there is a curious item included: a Rolls Royce bonnet bearing an unusual mascot. Because of his hurdling career my father had to have two artificial hip joints fitted, one, in the early days of such operations, in 1953, and the other in 1960. Owing to his cracking the cement in the second when riding to hounds, a replacement was necessary. He then had the previous prosthesis crested and mounted as a mascot on the bonnet of his Rolls Royce. Years later, I met the man who engraved the hip with the family crest above the words 'To a loyal supporter, 1960–1970'. The jeweller said that in all his years serving behind the counter he had never had such a peculiar request.

When my parents travelled abroad to places like Yugoslavia they would pull up at petrol stations or customs posts and a chattering group of small boys would gather, first to look at the numberplate AAA1 (conveniently standing for Amateur Athletic Association) and then at the curious surreal object on the bonnet. Finally they would look at my mother laid out and sedated on the back seat to protect her nerves from my father's excessive speeding, and that convinced them that they were dealing with true English eccentrics.

When returning from Sister Agnes's Hospital after one of his hip operations, my father, now himself a passenger, was subject to rather a surprise. He came home in a very smooth Mercedes ambulance paid for with some slight agonizing by my mother, so it must have been very expensive. It pulled up on the south front of the house so as to decant him near his bedroom and fell straight through the paving slabs up to the axles, nearly depositing him among his stock of Médoc Supérieur in the cellar. For years we drank this awful wine for which he never paid more than a pound a bottle on principle. Almost anything which wiped out the stock would have been welcome.

Once past all the memorabilia the visitor comes to the eighteenth century: Capability Brown's Orangery, known to everyone as the 'caff'. It is a superb room in which to take a restoring cup of tea and reflect on the good fortune that has enabled the treasures in this most beautiful of houses to survive, and to hope that the future will deal kindly with the building and those who make their homes here.

*The hip replacement in situ*

# CHAPTER FIVE

# THE GROUND FLOOR

THE GROUND FLOOR ROOMS at Burghley are the private family apartments and are not open to the public. But these rooms are as historic as the State Rooms on the first floor and have also required many decisions about redecoration. Here, as elsewhere, we have been enormously helped by the inventories, which are one of Burghley's great strengths. Dated 1688, 1690, 1738 and 1763 they are consulted regularly when we are trying to work out how the rooms were used in the past, how they were furnished, and to extract vital information on the acquisition of goods.

One of the things I most enjoy at Burghley is sitting by a blazing fire on a November evening, the room garnished with snoring dogs, with the crackling, faded pages of the inventories written in the so-recognizable hands of long-gone Cecils and their employees (such as Culpepper Tanner) spread out on the floor.

## SCAGLIOLA HALL

IT WAS BECAUSE of the 1738 inventory that we were able to recreate the decoration of our front hall. Facing north, it is one of the splendid architectural rooms influenced by Capability Brown and Robert Adam. It is oblong in shape, with arched entrances at either end, two mahogany doors out onto the terraces, and doors into the library and dining room. The floor is a 'pavement' of gold, white and black marbles. The skirting boards are painted to resemble dark green serpentine, and when I first came here in 1956 the walls were covered in torn and faded dark red damask. The pilasters on the walls were painted white and had marble bases. The pilasters themselves sounded hollow when knocked, and so were obviously not marble. We were helped in identifying what they were made of because in the invaluable inventory this room is described as 'The Scagliola Hall'.

Scagliola is a material made from powdered selenite mounted onto gesso, and coloured and polished to imitate marble. It is mentioned by the ninth Earl, in 1768, when he peevishly requests of his sister in a letter from abroad: 'If my pillars in the hall have stopped sweating, please ask Mr Bartoli to come back and polish them.' Here was the proof, if we needed any, that the hall had once been different. It had probably been got at, decoratively speaking, about 1910. Inspired by the clues, we began gingerly scraping away at the back of a pilaster where least visible close to the wall. Below the white paint was the most vivid glowing golden colour. Several pots of paint stripper later we were looking at a completely new room, with the result that the red walls had to go. Yellow pillars and wine-coloured walls were the stuff of nightmares. We put a cream and yellow damask of eighteenth-century design on the walls, touched up the skirting where generations of Hoovers and mops had chipped the paint, and re-covered the armchairs. This last act sometimes appears to have been an extravagance as the chairs usually spend the winter months totally shrouded in waterproof coats, tweed caps and the like.

As usual we were very grateful to the excellent Gainsborough Silk Weaving Company whose textiles look absolutely correct in an historic interior. The man who has masterminded almost all our renovations for the last few years is a talented and patient interior designer from Stamford called Terry Spiller. He is used to spending long hours wading through colour samples and fabric swatches to help us try to find an affordable 'dirty green' or 'faded blue'. Everything comes down to cost in the end, and we are always in a state of shock when we realize how many metres of material will be required for curtains. As in the rooms upstairs, the scale of patterns has to be big enough.

## FAMILY DINING ROOM

THE FAMILY DINING ROOM leads off the Scagliola Hall and at one time was known as 'The Stone Parlour'. The floor is indeed made from beautiful soft grey limestone, cut into octagons. This room is north facing, which, coupled with the stone flooring, means that it is always cool. Because of this, it was ideal for use in hot weather in the eighteenth and early nineteenth centuries, when the main family dining room was on the south side of the house. It is worth considering that, wherever the family was eating, before electricity came to the house in 1956 they probably never had a hot meal because both rooms were at least 100 yards from the kitchens.

In many great houses, dining rooms are there to impress and to accommodate large groups of diners. I fear that the Cecils must have been an inhospitable lot, or else used the great hall for big parties, because we cannot fit many more than twenty in this room, and that is only by squashing them up on tiny chairs and eating with elbows well tucked in. But it must be pointed out that this room was created by the ninth Earl in the 1780s when it was not the fashion to entertain on the grand scale. It was the Elizabethans before him and the Victorians after him who went in for that.

The tenth Earl used the room for his wood-turning lathe, made by the firm of Holtzappfel, which made everything from billiard balls to banisters. Jon Culverhouse, our House Manager, found the instrument lurking under heaps of pigeon droppings in the old brew house, and it was one of the eighteenth-century highlights of our 1986 scientific instrument exhibition.

Today a glorious tapestry made by John Vanderbank covers one wall. To sit and look at this during a lull in the mealtime conversation is no hardship. Full of fat cherubs leaping about in the altogether, forging arrows for Cupid amid lush green and blue foliage, it is a delight. The large paintings on either side of the fireplace are by Melchior d'Hondecoeter: spaniels pursue ducks and other wildfowl, and there are exotic birds in a landscape. Over the mantelpiece a group of *The Family Pets*, by an anonymous artist, includes two most endearing guinea pigs.

My mother rescued a pair of carved black and gilded eighteenth-century blackamoors from where they had been banished upstairs and placed them at either end of the room in two convenient niches. In fact, they fit so well I rather wonder if the ninth Earl did not order them for these spaces and the Victorians took them out. They have been to David Hordern to be restored, as sadly someone had attacked them with a paint brush and the original lustre was horribly covered over, as well as the gilding having been 'improved'. The culprit was probably my grandfather who was never a shy restorer.

## LIBRARY AND ANTE-LIBRARY

ON THE OTHER side of the Scagliola Hall from the Family Dining Room lie the Library and Ante-Library. These were also created by the ninth Earl. He was a great bibliophile and amassed a handsome collection of books and bindings, many bound in Stamford binderies. The Earl furnished both rooms in the classical idiom, which included ordering two large gilded mirrors from Ince and Mayhew, who had to send to France for the glass plates. Below these stood two commodes, now in the dining room, also made by Ince and Mayhew, which echoed in the inlaid mahogany the swag design from the mirror frames.

My office is in the Ante-Library and, like most people, I am gradually sinking under the weight of accumulated paper. It is something of a culture shock to come from the rest of the house into here and find a computer, fax machine and photocopier, but I cannot imagine how I worked without them. The wooden pilasters which opened and had shelves of gilded volumes inside are now empty on the advice of our conservator. All the bookshelves in here and the library next door have had to be drilled with holes to allow air to pass freely. The leather bindings suffered terribly from the effects of the gas lighting and it has reduced some to crumbly sandwiches, held together with rather saucy bows.

The Library is used a great deal in the winter for shooting teas and trustees meetings. With a fire crackling away in the hearth and all the glowing crimson, green and brown books, it is a really cosy room to sit in. A journalist once wrote in the *Sunday Express*: 'Lady Victoria's library is furnished with a red and green fabric which would be hideous in a normal house.' I was not absolutely certain whether I had escaped condemnation.

## SPARE BEDROOMS

UNLIKE MANY HOUSES, our best spare bedrooms are on the ground floor. This is partly because of the re-organizations in the seventeenth century to emulate the contemporary French fashion of having 'His and Hers' suites separated by a central hall.

The fifth Earl slept in what is now called the Blue and Silver Bedroom. It was once a blue and gold room, because of the brilliant Soho tapestries heavily embroidered in gold thread on a blue ground which hung in here. Disaster struck about a hundred years after they were made in 1685, when they went to London to be cleaned. Some ignorant person stripped the gold covering off the silver thread, which promptly tarnished and went black. We now have tapestries which are a mere echo of their former selves, which is sad.

Traditionally this room has been rather dark and gloomy because it has a huge four-poster bed made by Ince and Mayhew 'in the antique style' for the ninth Earl. To rectify this we have set the curtains back in the window bay as far as we can and made them draw around the sides so as not to obstruct the light. One of the biggest problems in a house of this kind is how to light the very high rooms like this that have an ornate ceiling. In desperation we have sometimes resorted to strip lighting concealed in a cornice, or, as in this case, hidden it on top of the four-poster.

Adjacent to the bedroom is a dressing room, that splendid retreat for inebriated husbands or those who were 'non speaks' with their spouses, and beyond that a bathroom. It has a huge Victorian bath on splendid curly legs and a mahogany thunder box. It was from this northwest corner of the building that the long library wing used to protrude, part of the original 'E' design of the house to flatter the Queen, and it may have joined on at this bathroom, the very end room. When we came in 1982 the dressing room and bathroom were decorated with a printed linen of about 1904. Damp and gas had done their worst, but we were lucky to find in Terry's fabric samples a chintz duplicate in the original cheery colours. This has been hung, with the aid of that splendid modern device the staple gun, and has rejuvenated the two rooms.

In the seventeenth century the fifth Earl would have slept in the present-day bedroom, used the dressing room as such, and perhaps washed, if at all, in what is the current bathroom. On the other side of the bedroom was the Earl's 'anty roome' and another closet, and we have turned these into another spare suite. These rooms were all designed to run one into another so it has proved complicated adapting them for modern usage. I always have to caution guests to have very quiet rows and be fearfully polite about other couples because, with only a door between the bedrooms, every word carries.

The suites for the Earl and Countess occupied the whole of the west wing of the ground floor, and were separated by the vaulted stone West

*Blue and Silver Bedroom*

Entrance Hall. When they wished to see one another they would have had to walk across the hall, through his or her 'anty roome' before reaching the bedroom. Goodness knows how many servants would have been encountered *en route*, but it does not sound very cosy.

The decoration of these rooms described in the 1688 inventory was obviously quite something. 'My Lord's Roome' was hung with 'Aurora Damask' (a rosy pink colour), his 'closett' or bathroom with 'Indian Crimson and Gold Stuff', and the bedroom as it is now with 'Three paires of blue and gold hangings by Vanderbanc'. 'My Lady's Dressing Roome', as one might expect, was also pretty lavish: 'hung with Crimson

Damask and Indian Flowered Silk. Chairs with the same silk, black frames and crimson silk covers.' Her 'closett' was decorated in 'greene figured velvett, and silk fringe, easie chaire and 2 stooles, right Japan frames and the same greene velvett. Greene serge covers,' and the 'walnut tree writing table with silver sand box and standish in itt, inlayd as the floor is.'

In the closet alone, there were forty-seven pictures, quite a lot of them miniatures, mostly of religious subjects, and some unframed. Several of the pictures and decorative items listed in the inventory also occur in Culpepper Tanner's accounts for purchases made on the visits to Italy. And, just as today we would display a souvenir of a successful holiday, Anne placed her new acquisitions where she could see them everyday. On her closet mantelpiece stood 'Two wt [white – *blanc de chine*] criples' and 'two wt nunns; Two silver flower spriggs from Milan; A Daphne and Apollo in Ivory on a pedistall of Ebony and carved.'

## WEST ENTRANCE HALL

BETWEEN THE 'HIS AND HERS' suites is the West Entrance Hall. It is no longer used as an entrance because the continual westerly winds catch the curtains, sending them billowing disastrously over neighbouring porcelain, slam distant doors and generally put all and sundry out of sorts. The hall is now a calm place, fronted by the stupendous but rusting golden gates forged by Jean Tijou in about 1685. They were last gilded in my father's time. It was not a successful foray into conservation; new aluminium acanthus leaves did not like having gold leaf stuck all over them, which resulted in a chicken-pox like appearance, with white excrescences. Sooner rather than later it will all have to be replaced with wrought iron and new gold leaf. The last estimate we had for this work was about £50,000. Not the sort of sum that is ready to hand.

The drab walls of the hall once had decorations by Antonio Verrio and in a certain light you can still see the ghostly figures, floral garlands and wheat sheaves. Everything was lost when, in an attack of medievalism, the second Marquess scrubbed the walls to make them look more ancient and in keeping with the original groined stone ceiling which bore (and still bears) his ancestor's proud inscription, 'W. DOM de BURGHLEY. 1577'.

Also on the ceiling is a selection of early heraldic shields with minimal decoration, a sign of good, old lineage. When my son was at prep school, he once innocently enquired of another boy what his family crest was. After a short pause the answer came back: 'Our family is so old we don't have a crest; our shield is blank.' Richard was terribly impressed.

Plumbing was an abiding interest for past generations and none more so than my father's. In 1956, for reasons unknown except to himself, he installed in this hall a powerful, automatically flushing urinal within concrete housing. It had the disadvantage of showering male guests with water and frightening them half to death when at their most vulnerable. It also caused them acute embarrassment when they had to request a visit to a normal appliance, which inevitably was shuttered, dark and icy cold. The first thing we did after installing the 'Little Chef' next door was to put in an ordinary loo.

## BLUE DRAWING ROOM

Leading on from 'My Lady's Closett' is the Blue Drawing Room. In earlier times it was a reception room, subsequently a bedroom and then the family sitting room, which is how I have always known it. My parents made it into a very individual room by covering the walls in a cheerful yellow wallpaper and putting up a massive run of Utility shelving which contained almost every 'Penguin' thriller ever published and an excellent set of Surtees's novels, as well as various art books such as Bénézit's dictionary of artists and catalogues of exhibitions featuring seventeenth-century paintings.

Above the bookshelves hung two paintings dubiously attributed to Claude and between these a landscape enthusiastically attributed to Gainsborough, its thick coating of rich yellow varnish adding to the ancient aura and disguising Dr Happ's over-enthusiastic restoration. On every flat surface there were countless models of foxes, horses and hounds made from every sort of material: porcelain, pottery, lead and bronze. On the mantelpiece stood my father's collection of hunting horns, silver examples on one side and copper ones on the other, and on either side of the fireplace were the coaching horns, which from time to time he would blow very skilfully, mostly to annoy my mother.

My father would sit in an enormous red hide-covered chair which had spent part of its early life in the fishpond at our previous house in an attempt to soak out the salt which had got into the leather on a transatlantic voyage. It never looked quite normal after that but was extremely comfortable. My mother would perch under the light beside the fire in an attempt to see the tapestry she was working on. This was her great and abiding hobby, and during her lifetime she made about six large rugs, several chair and stool seats and a number of cushions. Travelling abroad with my father when he was engaged in his work for the International Olympic Committee, it was her 'tatting', I believe, which kept her sane. She spent many productive hours in this way when shut into her hotel bedroom while meetings went on in the sitting room of the suite they were given.

The friendships my father made all over the world through his work for the Olympic movement were very dear to him, and as a child I became used to guests turning up to dine or stay the night from Africa, Australia and even Russia. There would always be three Russians: one sports delegate, one translator (KGB) and one government representative. My mother used to say 'one on, one off and one in the wash'! They drank large amounts of beer and gave us all out-of-date Soviet sports' badges.

We once had an International Amateur Athletic Federation conference at Burghley. One of the most charming delegates was an American called Dan Ferris. He was small, round, funny, slightly vague and short-sighted. One day we saw from the terrace the unmistakable Dan outline down by the lake and this prompted another American to make this rather good remark to my father: 'Say, Dave, you've got Ferris at the bottom of your garden!'

The sitting room was the first room we tackled when we moved into Burghley; it was just too reminiscent of the old folks. The curtains, a riot of colour with hunting scenes of horsemen and hounds rollicking about, were totally rotten from too much sunshine and only extended down to the window sill. I am not the first person to be appalled by the drop needed for curtains in this house. We were lucky that a cancelled order provided us with just enough ivory cotton damask to do a proper job, right down to the floor; curiously, we subsequently found that in the 1688 inventory the curtains in this room were described as 'white damask'...

The Penguin books went upstairs with the other books and that took us a whole weekend of heavy lifting and carrying. We then took out the shelving and decided to hang the walls in blue silk, completely unaware

*My father and mother in their sitting room, now the Blue Drawing Room*

that since records were kept this room has always been blue. Because of our love for Kakiemon porcelain we had a carpet designed with the same colours in it.

## RED DRAWING ROOM

NEXT TO THE Blue Drawing Room is the rather posher Red Drawing Room. This is very much a room with which to impress visitors, although not an impossible size to live in. The decoration has not been changed since the nineteenth century. The ceiling is finely decorated

*The author in the*
*Blue Drawing Room*

with garlands of fruit and flowers, a smoky grey colour picked out in gold leaf. The walls are covered in a rosy striped silk which makes a marvellous background on which to hang the superb paintings.

On the west wall is one of the great treasures of the house: *The Adoration of the Magi* by Jacopo Bassano. On either side of it we have hung the two standing saints by Paolo Veronese which were the original organ doors in the church of San Giacomo in Murano, bought from Lord Halifax by the ninth Earl, and brought back here, together with the chapel altarpiece, in the eighteenth century.

*The Virgin at Prayer* by Sassoferrato hangs on the back of the door to the passage, above which hangs *Susanna and the Elders* by Artemisia Gentileschi. This picture was recently described by an American author as a copy, but as she has done no research in the Burghley archives nor actually seen the painting in question I feel it a rather limp piece of academic de-attribution.

The large mirror over the fire was, when made in 1768, the biggest sheet of glass produced in England. It was almost certainly made at the Vauxhall works of the Duke of Buckingham and is a monster. Even if we are forced to redecorate one day we shall, with luck, not have to take it down; the fragility of the gilded Ince and Mayhew frame makes me feel quite weak.

One of John Bly's greatest restoration successes is in this room. It is a cabinet on stand and for years was called the Rubens cabinet because of the skilfully painted mythological scenes painted on the copper plates on the drawers and doors. The whole piece was in an appalling state when we came in 1982, because for ages it had stood over the central heating pipe and was riddled with woodworm, which had virtually destroyed both ends and the top. These were held together by one or two remaining flakes of ebony veneer and the tortoiseshell which covered the carcase between the drawers and the metal mounts and hinges. John had to remove the veneer and remake the carcase, filling the woodworm damage on those bits that could be saved and replacing others. The copper panels were removed for cleaning and were found to be signed on the back by someone nobody had ever heard of, with sadly not a trace of Rubens.

When the beautiful Aubusson carpet of about 1810 went away to be cleaned and repaired, we found the original eighteenth-century carpet underneath, being used as underfelt. Scarlet, gold and black, the pattern exactly matched the carving on the ceiling. We could not bear to throw it out, so it is still the underfelt.

## MARBLE HALL

ESIGNED AS A COUNTERPOINT to the Scagliola Hall is the Marble Hall, so-called because of the marble floor and its collection of marble statues in the seventeenth century. The two halls are approximately opposite one another, with the centre courtyard between them. This hall, however, is much less imposing, especially as one of the objects it was supposed to house was a lyrical and skilfully conceived marble statue by Monnot of Andromeda chained to a rock, which was bought for £300 in 1680 by the fifth Earl. Unfortunately it had to be sold to help pay death duties in 1956 and is now in the Metropolitan Museum of Art in New York.

Of all the rooms in the house this works the least well for today's lifestyle. We do not need another sitting room and in any case the four doors provide draughts from four directions and, by virtue of the panelling, it is extremely dark. Set into the wood are portraits of various ancestors, all the women conforming to the protruding-eye style from the age of Kneller and Lely.

## SOUTH DINING ROOM

THE SOUTH DINING ROOM was abandoned long ago as a place to eat (see Family Dining Room p.201). My mother used it as a storeroom for grandchildren's toys. For a dance in 1964, it was satisfactorily turned into a night club done out as a garden room. Stripped of furniture except for cane chairs and tables, and with two swing seats and fake grass on the floor, it was highly successful. The only slightly bizarre thing about the room was that when, in due course, the fake grass wore out, my mother quite calmly put down some more. It looked a trifle queer with the gilt mahogany furniture and massive oak sideboard, but it does mean that we are probably the only second-generation fake-grass household in the country.

*(overleaf) Aerial view from the northeast*

# CHAPTER SIX

# THE PARK AND GARDENS

## THE OUTBUILDINGS AND THE GARDENS

A HOUSE LIKE BURGHLEY does not stand in isolation. There are numerous outbuildings, courtyards, stables and workshop areas. In the past these buildings contained the slaughter-house, the brewhouse, the bakehouse, the dairy, the tack room, the stables themselves, the linenroom, the wash house, coach houses, garages, the servants' ballroom, staff flats and houses, and the men's rooms, used for unmarried staff.

Today the stores contain paint, putty, timber, electric cable, plugs, bulbs, old Aga cookers, baths, sinks, kitchen units, loos, copper piping, poly piping, glass, woodworm killer and all the other thousand things necessary for the maintenance not only of Burghley itself but of all the estate properties. The forge, the painters' shop, the carpenter's workshop and the stonemason's shop were and are a constant scene of renovation in progress.

The office where the general day-to-day organization is handled, and all enquiries relating to the house opening, is run by the House Manager Jon Culverhouse, his wife Sarah, and a trainee assistant. It is perhaps surprising that there is no recognized course at any college or a grant-aided scheme to train private country-house curators, but a year's practical experience, which we are rather good at providing, is worth a lot of theory. Not every house could handle this sort of scheme but Jon is a very remarkable person. When he came for his interview in 1984, Michael Scott and I had seen about forty candidates. Jon's name came in right at the end, but the moment he and Sarah appeared we knew our search was over. I could not have coped with the job I do here without Jon; besides, he is the only person who knows how to edit what I write on the computer.

*The House, Estate and Estate Office staff in 1992*

Other staff include Alan Scott, the Estate Clerk of Works; Trevor and Dean, painters; Ken the electrician; Tony, John and Mervyn, joiners; Gwyn the stonemason; Carl the blacksmith; Des the semi-retired carpenter; the tilers Maurice, Lawrence, Eddie and Simon; and Viv the ex-plumber, who knows where the drains are. The security of the house, of paramount importance, is taken care of by Steve, Bill and Jack. There are eight employees in the Orangery, twelve guides, four shop ladies, two exhibition supervisors, four cleaners, one of whom cleans eighteen state rooms and manages the linen room and three who clean the family quarters part time, a cook, and a butler and his assistant. The Estate Office is manned by Sir Giles Floyd, Michael Scott, Ken Woolley, our accountant Ian Graham, Mrs Farrow and Sonia Archdale.

It is, of course, inevitable that however many people are employed, there are always jobs to do in a place like this. We all muck in and do things far outside the neat and tidy job description. For example, one winter, after a severe snow storm, one of the roofs over the book store began to leak all over the newly installed folio racks and on down through

*Lancelot 'Capability' Brown by Nathaniel Dance
(Pagoda Room)*

*View of the house through the Lion Bridge, designed
by Capability Brown (1775)*

the next ceiling onto the ground floor. Having discovered the leak, I notified Jon and, together with Charles, his assistant, we clambered out onto the roof to deal with the problem. This particular area is only accessible by exiting through a small window. While we busily shovelled snow out of the gutters, there was a gust of wind and the window blew shut behind us. There was no catch on the outside.

An hour later, with blue hands and noses, we had shouted 'help' until we were hoarse and the light was fading. Charles, as the youngest and fittest, had been unanimously elected the chap to go over the top and crawl onto the higher roof level and yell from there. No joy. All those who dwell in the Chestnut Yard were safely ensconced in front of their televisions with steaming mugs of tea. What to do? By now we were slightly losing our senses of humour but hope loomed. We could see, at a very oblique angle down on the ground floor, the very top of the pantry window. After several vain attempts we managed a sneaky backhanded snowball, which burst in a satisfactory fashion against the window above the pantry sink. The assistant butler heard the frenzied cries accompanying the missile and, thank goodness, came out to investigate. 'Good God' he exclaimed, on spotting the three anxious faces up on the roof. 'What are you doing up there?' I explained that we were sweeping the roof free of snow. 'I thought we had somebody to do that', he remarked, as he began the weary climb to let us escape.

In addition to our own staff, NADFAS, the National Association of Decorative and Fine Art Societies, has been of invaluable help. Two local groups, from Peterborough and Leicester, provide excellent support by guiding on Sundays. In the future we hope to involve the ladies in book conservation. Houses like this can only operate with a great deal of local goodwill. The common bond between all those who are occupied here is that they are devoted to the house itself and want to see it flourish.

We feel very strongly that there is no place for empty buildings and, within our budget, are aiming to turn as much unused property into productive space as possible. Stables not occupied by horses are currently in use as a book bindery, run by Blair Jeary, and a picture conservation studio where Michael Cowell is in charge. The latter has worked on a huge number of paintings, as well as preparing a photographic record of the work still to be done before we can relax. Michael's wife Chris is a gilder; so all we need now is a furniture restorer, a porcelain restorer and a textile workshop and we will have a complete set-up here.

It is not very innovative to have used the buildings in this way; many houses have done something similar, but the principle of people renting workshops close by the consumer who will use their skills, at times mutually convenient, is very satisfactory.

In the bottom or lower yard are the old stables where Gillies confined his brood mares. Sadly these are in a state of disrepair at present and occupied by chickens. During the day these ramble happily among the public, sharing picnics and greeting visitors. We had one driver of a fifty-seven seater coach who refused to let his passengers off because, eyeing the Rhode Island Red perched cosily on the bus step, he said, 'You can never tell with hens, they can be very nasty when roused'.

The forge, used on a regular basis by Carl Zimmerman, and scene of so many happy childhood days, is down here. Carl, with Des the semi-retired carpenter, is busy making over 300 stainless steel windows for the house to replace the rusted eighteenth-century iron frames. No two windows measure the same so it is a painstaking task.

The old store yielded a treasure-trove a few years ago when Jon found thousands of ceramic glazed floor tiles, dating we think from the seventeenth century. Heaped in serried ranks, they measure about eight inches across and are decorated in yellows and greens. In the 1688 inventory a 'Tile Roome' is mentioned. Perhaps this store contains the discarded tiles from that time.

Beyond lies the carpenter's old store and the stonemason's workshop. There is a full-time programme of repairs to the stonework around the house stretching into infinity. Gwyn Watkins is our stonemason now and his dust-whitened countenance is to be seen at all hours, either terrifyingly perched up on a chimney or chiselling away in the shop.

The lower yard also leads to the gardens. This is where a great deal of activity is now taking place. With the expertise of Elizabeth Banks we have undertaken a full appraisal of the 'pleasure grounds' and gardens. Their history goes back a long way. John Gerard, a notable Elizabethan herbalist and gardener laid out the gardens at Theobalds, Lord Burghley's other house, but we do not know if he did the same at Burghley. In the seventeenth century, London and Wise, the leading garden designers, from Kensington, worked for the fifth Earl and created one of the greatest and most fashionable pleasure grounds ever made. The pleached-lime walks, the ponds, the bleaching grounds, the parterres, and the sunken lawns and terraces stretched as far as the eye could see. We know all this

*The author with her husband, Simon, and their children, Miranda and Richard*

*(opposite) View of the house from the southwest*

from a photograph of the plan of the garden in 1755, just before Lancelot 'Capability' Brown was employed by the ninth Earl to modernize and countrify the design. Brown was paid £1,000 per annum for a period of twenty-three years, at the end of which they parted on mutually fed-up terms.

Capability Brown was raised in Northumberland, a county of open spaces, architectural trees, and water. He brought all these influences with him to Burghley, creating a 'river', in reality a serpentine lake, from the original ponds. These stew ponds, dating from the time of the old priory, had no doubt been used by the first Lord Burghley and his mother as a fresh supply of fish. There is a seam of blue clay which exactly follows the line of the present lake and is ideal for puddling the base of a lake or pond to make it leak proof. It is, however, a terrible material to have in a garden; cracking in summer, cold and sticky in winter. The hill, known as the mount, to the southeast of the house is made from it, being the spoil from Capability's lake. To date it has defeated efforts to sustain attractive plants, although shrub roses and some trees survive grudgingly. Under Capability Brown's scheme boathouses sprang up on the bank of the lake, and a shrubbery, with grass walks between walls of flowering species, was made on the east slope which was the far side of the mount from the house. All the seventeenth-century conceits were swept away in this new design, leaving the garden composed of trees, shrubs and acres of grass.

Perhaps we should be grateful for the lesser upkeep needed for such a plan, but as a keen and plants-orientated gardener I weep for what was taken away. The Victorians had a stab at amenity horticulture, installing here and there terracotta urns made by Blashfield and Co. in Stamford. They also installed a fine boathouse on the far side of the lake made by the same manufacturer. They planted specimen trees but sadly did not keep up Capability's shrubbery, which I suppose probably finally disappeared during World War II when there were no staff. I blush to admit that the laurels, swept away when we came in 1982 as being a Victorian leftover, were certainly the last stragglers originating from the eighteenth century. Elizabeth Banks is advising us on the replanting and planning of the shrubbery. It will, as far as we can make it, follow in design and content the original Brown installation. It is going to be a long-term and expensive exercise.

We plan to open the gardens on a regular basis for people to see them

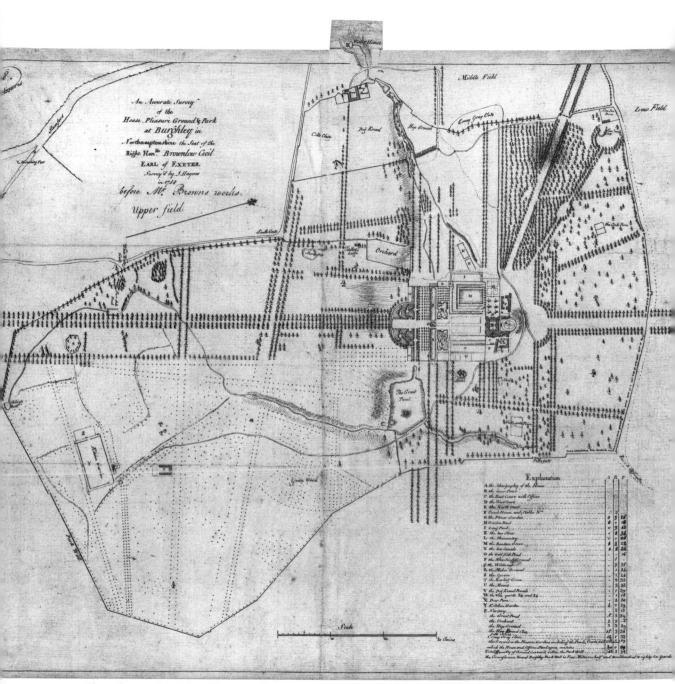

*Plan drawn by John Haynes in 1755 prior to Capability Brown's alterations (Collection Centre Canadien d'Architecture/Canadian Centre for Architecture, Montréal)*

from conception to adulthood, as it were. We hope to keep the thirty-five acres of lawn and plantings up to a good standard in spite of having only three and a half gardeners, instead of the eight who were employed when my parents came, and the thirty or so who were working under Capability Brown.

It would be hard to admit that a house as great as Burghley did not boast a commensurate garden, and hopefully this historical reconstruction will raise our horticultural image and attract the same support from the press and visitors as we receive for the house.


## THE PARK

BURGHLEY STANDS within an ancient park, dating back to the days of Church ownership before the house was in existence. We know little about the way in which it was farmed or planted until the seventeenth century. In 1623 the park and gardens together made 448 acres. We have been told that some of the oldest surviving lime trees (*Tilia cordata*, pre 1623) in England are to be found in the original avenues leading from the house to the Great North Road. These avenues were incorporated by Capability Brown in his grandiose planting schemes for the ninth Earl. Purchase of more land by the tenth Earl in 1796 increased the park to 1400 acres.

Inevitably, trees have to be felled and replaced from time to time – an agonizingly slow procedure. The descendants of the original Tudor herd of fallow deer graze the park and afford visitors enormous pleasure, except in the rutting season, when the bucks fight one another and occasionally forget themselves and have a go at a passer-by. There is a long tradition of this; a bill from a merchant in the eighteenth century claims medical costs after being 'Gored by a stag in Burghley Park'. Today the deer are lovingly cared for by George Seymour.

Beyond the walls of the lower park lies Stamford, arguably the most beautiful town in England. Built of the same silver limestone as Burghley, it has five medieval churches, unspoilt eighteenth-century streets and one of the oldest coaching inns in the country; an architectural gem.

Despite the difficulties between the house and the town in the time of the second Marquess, there has been a very close relationship in recent years. We are united in trying to fight off the proposed scheme to by-pass the town through the park. The road is badly needed because of the heavy traffic which goes through Stamford, but, nonetheless, most people value the peace of Burghley Park too highly to endorse such a scheme and would rather see the road go elsewhere.

## BURGHLEY HORSE TRIALS

BURGHLEY IS PART OF an historical sporting estate. For generations, since the house itself grew from the remains of St Michael's Priory, the woods and grassland within the park and nearby policies have been used to provide food for the household and estate: rabbits, hares, pheasants and deer. All part of a countryside pattern which has survived to the present day. The farming of bygone years was more tolerant of raiding rabbits and hungry hares than we are now; in fact we reluctantly regard them as vermin.

Cub hunting marks the end of the summer. In the old days, when my father was still hunting hounds, the first day's cubbing took place on the Saturday of the Horse Trials. At about 6 a.m. we would meet outside the kennels in the park and set off for the first draw in the Butlands about half a mile away. The air would still be full of the night's mist gradually being burnt off by the sun, the rides in the wood were lined with blackberries and huge cobwebs covered the grass.

The unusual thing about this particular meet were the people who came: all the top British competitors in the Event as well as Polish, Russian, French, German and Italian riders, and of course the Irish team who made the whole thing very jolly. Most of the foreign horses were rather amazed by the hounds, those more accustomed just became unbearably excited, occasionally performing airborne manoeuvres not dreamt of by dressage afficionados, to the amusement of those watching.

It was splendidly laid-back and emotional to see these terribly fit horses and riders, the best in the world at their sport, standing with the rest of us outside the covert, being yelled at by Papa and taking off like the wind to turn the young hounds from a hare or deer. Later they would risk everything over a cross-country course in front of thousands of people, having already completed the first two parts of the second day's events – a steeplechase, and the roads and tracks section. The true spirit of sportsmen, willing to have a go at whatever was on offer.

*My father with HM The Queen and HRH Princess Margaret at the 1967 Horse Trials*

Following the cross-country section on the Saturday many of the riders would come to church in St Martin's on the Sunday, where we would have a suitably equine sermon preached in double-quick time by the vicar, Albert Irwin, who was extremely conscious of my father's views on long drawn out harangues.

When Albert Irwin came to the parish he inherited from the previous incumbent a machine manufactured to the highest standards by A. C. Cossors, of whom Papa was a director. It sat ominously on the edge of the pulpit. Whoever was preaching had to set it by turning a key; a green light would come on, followed after eight minutes by a red light and after ten minutes by a buzzer, which reduced more than one garrulous clergyman to a state of nervous anticipation and almost prevented them uttering at all. Albert proved himself to be such a master of the swift message that the instrument was thrown away. There have been times when we have regretted its passing since he retired.

The happy old days of the early Horse Trials have, of course, gone forever. Nowadays the competing animals are so valuable that their owners, however willing, could not contemplate taking them out for a morning's hunting just before an event. The stakes are higher; the prize money has gone up and it is no longer sufficient just to compete. You have to be in the ribbons in order to win enough to somehow pay the forage bills, the vet's bills, the groom's wages and the fees to enable you to enter further top class competitions. And if you do well it will please your sponsor, if you have one, or your mother if you don't.

The Burghley Event has always held a special place in the eventing

*The author and Captain Mark Phillips (course designer) at the 1991 Burghley Horse Trials (Courtesy of Eventing Magazine)*

calendar. It is one of two premier horse trials held in Britain. The other is Badminton. It takes place in September when we can almost guarantee good weather. For the last few years we have in fact been plagued by drought, which on this very light free-draining soil causes the track to become very hard. Every year we spend more and more time, effort, and money trying to ensure that the going is as good as it can possibly be. We pump water out of Capability Brown's lake onto the turf, which makes the lake smell most peculiar and puts the geese in a rage. It greens up the grass in a jiffy but it takes us all year to replace the extracted water unless we have a good wet winter. We also lay hundreds of tons of silt and sand on the take off and landing points at each obstacle.

The tens of thousands of people who support the Event come for a variety of reasons, everything from doing their Christmas shopping at some of the marvellous shops in 'Burghley Bond Street' to following the progress of a friend who is riding in every discipline: dressage, cross country and finally show jumping. There are those wanting to buy a good horse who watch closely for a promising youngster: those wanting to sell a horse, perhaps to trade up into proven talent. Families attend with numerous children who get lost, copious picnics and vast numbers of dogs. The whole performance is splendidly tweedy and countrified, without any of the false socializing which characterizes other horsey happenings.

The number of farmers, hunt staff, Pony Club members and local helpers for the Burghley Event is astonishing. I was about to say staggering, but since an edict was issued by the governing body of horse trials, ruling that no alcohol was to be consumed by any official, things have sobered up a bit. In fact, 1000 volunteer helpers work on producing the Trials, including 200 Stamford Round Tablers without whom the whole event would fall apart.

Once the show is over, the boring work of clearing up the litter begins. In spite of there being a team of 'picker-uppers' during the four days, it is surprising how much junk is left behind. Our particular problem is that two weeks later the herd of fallow deer is released into the park again having spent the previous month in captivity in a large pen. They are greedy and interested, so string and plastic are magnetic attractions. One year four died in agony as a result of carelessness and untidiness. It is a huge park but it must be cleared if this tragedy is not to be repeated.

# EPILOGUE

## THE TREASURE HOUSE AND ITS FUTURE

O F ALL THE great houses in Britain, Burghley has been one of the most blessed by the variety and quantity of works of art purchased by its inhabitants and in its possession. And there are no other houses where inventories of the contents have yielded so much information about how these items were acquired, when, by whom, and for how much.

From before the Elizabethan beginnings of the house there are some rare medieval documents. Tucked away at the back of a drawer in the muniments room, Sotheby's expert Christopher de Hamel found a small piece of fine vellum. It was a document, now considered an eleventh-century forgery, handing over to the Abbey of Peterborough lands at the neighbouring village of Walcot. It has small crosses embossed in bright gold on the left-hand side and, opposite, the supposed signature marks of Edward the Confessor (?1002–66) and of Harold II (?1022–66). We could, in fact, hold an exhibition of royal documents and charters of every reign from Edward the Confessor to Elizabeth I. There are ones from later reigns too, but it is the early period which is particularly fascinating.

The collection proper began with the Builder, Sir William Cecil. His possessions reflected his ability, thanks to a privileged position at court, to acquire the very best fine art. One example is the superb silver-gilt mounted Wanli ewer and basin sold in 1888 and now in the Metropolitan Museum of Art in New York. They were possibly a gift to him but might be the items mentioned in Sir Walter Ralegh's will as a gift to Sir William's second son, Robert Cecil. If it was the latter, then we have no idea how it came to Burghley, rather than Hatfield House. In either case it was a gift which would surely not have been given to someone who did not appreciate it to the full.

Another marvellous piece of Chinese blue-and-white porcelain fortunately eluded the auctioneer's hammer in the nineteenth century. It is a

231

*The forged charter granting land to the Abbey of Peterborough, with the supposed signature marks of Edward the Confessor and Harold II*

late-sixteenth-century lobed and silver-gilt mounted bowl, decorated with the 'Horses of Mu-Wang' round the rim and with panels of fruit, flowers and exotic birds round the sides. It was given by Queen Elizabeth I to her godson, Lord Walsingham, and it came to Burghley in 1731 as a gift of Lady Osborne to the eighth Earl. The bowl has been used ever since when family members have been christened. In these ecumenical times it pleases me that we use a Buddhist artefact for such an important Christian ceremony.

There is an intriguing footnote to the story of this bowl. In Drake's Bay, off the coast of America near San Francisco, some shards of blue-and-white porcelain were dredged up from the bottom of the sea. It is the place where Drake boarded a Spanish treasure ship and took the cargo of porcelain in the name of the Queen. Elizabeth no doubt kept some of the booty for herself, especially as she probably financed at least part of the voyage. The interesting point for us is that the discovered shards exactly match the bowl that we possess.

Dating also from the sixteenth century is the map drawn by John Dee which is inserted into Sir William Cecil's atlas. Maps by Dee are extremely rare and Burghley is fortunate to possess this example. Dee was a scholar at St John's College, Cambridge at the same time as Cecil and later became noted as an alchemist, mathematician and geographer, whose skill at mapmaking was no doubt of enormous benefit to Elizabethan sailors. He published seventy-nine books dealing with logic, mathematics, astrology, alchemy and navigation, and was a great collector of books himself. Dee was regarded with great suspicion by the general public, who accused him of necromancy and all manner of wizardry. Matters were not helped by Dee's attachment to his assistant Edward Kelley, a rogue who pretended to be in touch with the spirit world, and duped Dee into believing he had found the elixir of life at Glastonbury, among other things. Public opinion was so strong against Dee that his house and library were sacked by a crowd, and thousands of priceless incunabulae and books were thrown into the Thames. Dee was even imprisoned at one point in his career: accused of causing the death of Mary I by sorcery in 1558.

The late seventeenth century was the period of the house's great flowering. As we have seen, money was no object to the fifth Earl and Countess, and it was combined with good taste and an inclination for foreign travel. Italy and France lay there like artistic larders, and the couple came home laden with loot. Their delight in the grandiose flower pieces available in Italy at that time is reflected in the two large (10 feet by 6 feet) paintings by Giuseppe Recco, a Neapolitan master, which hang in the Third George Room. It is interesting that at a time when most English aristocrats would display their foreign purchases at their smart London houses, to impress their friends and visitors with their wealth and sophistication, John and Anne were content to buy over three hundred pictures specifically for the beautification of a remote country house to be enjoyed almost entirely by the family alone. I wonder if they ever considered the generations to come; I suspect not at all.

The entry for the North Drawing Room, on the ground floor, in the

1688 inventory refers to '1 inlaid large french cabinett, gueridons, table and stand to it.' This is easily identified as the Pierre Gôle suite now in the Blue Silk Bedroom. The couple seemed to be fond of 'cabinetts' for there are eight described in the inventory, including the 'Right Japan and mother of pearl' version (now in the Red Drawing Room), one in 'Primrose wood' and two mentions of 'hardstone cabinetts' on stands, presumably the Florentine cabinets now in the Heaven Room. There is no reason to suppose that any of these items were in the house before John and Anne went shopping. There must have been a tremendous disposal of ancient and outmoded furniture in this period. When Culpepper Tanner found things that seemed past their best he invariably described them in the inventory as 'worn' or 'old'. The only Elizabethan items still extant at that time might be a 'paire of formes' in the Great Hall, together with '24 fire bucketts and the fire engin and a cedar raille'.

The amount of time and money spent on improvements to the building in the period 1674–1700 cannot be stressed enough. If it took us 3,000 man hours to restore the Laguerre walls and ceiling in the Bow Room, one can scarcely imagine how long the artist and his helpers spent on the design, the preparation of the surfaces, and then the final painting. This labour had been echoed in the George Rooms by Verrio, and an unknown army of other artisans was occupied in other disciplines, such as woodwork, metalwork and glazing, throughout this period, to create usable rooms out of the Elizabethan galleries and spaces.

Nearly all the collections that we enjoy and marvel at today were either bought, or acquired by deed of gift, in this period, or during the life of the ninth Earl in the eighteenth century. Many objects and paintings have, of course, been added to the house in subsequent generations, but the core of the collections date from 1674–1700. The only major category of works of art not represented in the collection is old master drawings. A few unattributed ones are mentioned in the 1688 inventory, but it appears to be a field in which the couple was not interested.

That John and Anne were proud of Burghley goes without saying, that they loved it is highly probable, and that it was their life's work is without question. It is remarkable that over 300 years, through two world wars, the ups and downs of personal fortunes and the black days of taxation in the 1950s, their descendants have felt that it was important, where possible, to keep the collections intact, and whenever funds allowed, to go on embellishing the house as best they could.

In view of the years of effort and the affection shown to the house, I think this generation has no right to turn its back on a pre-eminent part of England's heritage. The house is not a dinosaur unable to survive in the modern world; it is a living classroom open to anyone with the inclination to learn, and also happens to be a family home. The thousands of visitors who pass through the State Rooms every year are pleasantly surprised by the atmosphere: 'it seems so friendly', 'what a lovely feeling it has', are typical remarks made to me.

It would be sad if future governments turned a blind eye to the predicament of owners struggling to preserve houses like Burghley for future generations of visitors and their own descendants. Government grants via English Heritage are hard to obtain, and, increasingly, reduced in size because they are spread over more and more buildings in need. In the last resort, where a house of exceptional importance is for sale, the government and other organizations, such as the National Heritage Memorial Fund, can step in and buy the property, which can then be run by the National Trust for Places of Historic Interest or Natural Beauty. However, the National Trust is not able to provide all the answers. Its resources are already stretched to the limit because, as the buildings in its care grow older, it has to carry out costly repairs from an income derived in many cases from farming, which is not as profitable as it once was. In any case, the National Trust would far rather see these houses remain in the care of responsible owners.

Having a motivated family working to keep up a property, with assistance from the government in the form of exemption from the sales tax VAT on repairs, would be a far cheaper solution than that of the government's having to fund the purchase and upkeep of such a house with a grant derived from the taxpayer. At present, an owner is expected to pay for repairs to his property out of earned income (on which he may have paid tax) and then to pay value added tax (VAT), levied in 1992 at 17.5 per cent, on those repairs. The tax component in the bill for three-quarters of an acre of lead roof is quite considerable. The sheer size and quantity of the repairs required for an old building grind the private owner down.

Five million overseas visitors visit historic properties in Britain each year, so these houses are making a positive contribution to the nation's tourist industry. Local towns, businesses, restaurants and shops also benefit. The owner charges the visitor to see round his house, but after providing guides, cloakroom facilities, security systems, ropes and signs, flowers, a car park, a cashier, and conserving and restoring the works of art on view, as well as the buildings and rooms used by the visitors, there will always be a substantial gap between expenditure and income, which has to be found elsewhere.

No one is suggesting that the government should be responsible for funding an outdated and luxurious lifestyle for private owners, but if, as a nation, we wish to preserve works of art in their original country-house setting, then some help will have to be forthcoming, particularly for the smaller house without resources.

I know of few owners who do not have the deep conviction that by continuing to live in their houses they are giving the building and contents the best chance of survival. Few can view the future with equanimity, but see no alternative to keeping going for as long as their finances allow.

The idea that behind every tree lurks a multi-millionaire with a bottomless pocket, longing to rescue an architectural gem and restore it to its full glory, does not appear to be based on reality. Those with the money to buy a 'stately home' soon discover that, however rich they are, the house will swallow all they have and more. In addition, the inconvenience of having to walk hundreds of yards a day, the cold rooms in winter, and the impossibility of obtaining and keeping good staff, tend to dull the original enthusiasm. In most cases, within a few years, the owners have gone bust and the property is back on the market. The increase in country-house hotels and golf hotels appears to have levelled off for the moment.

In the case of Burghley, thanks to my father's foresight in setting up the Burghley House Preservation Trust in 1969, this house and its contents will not be separated. The efforts of all the ancestors down the years have not been wasted, and the love and affection they lavished on this place will continue to be part of the future of this most beautiful of England's houses.

# INDEX

Figures in italics refer to captions